AF608329

URBAN SPELL

TORKIL GUDNASON

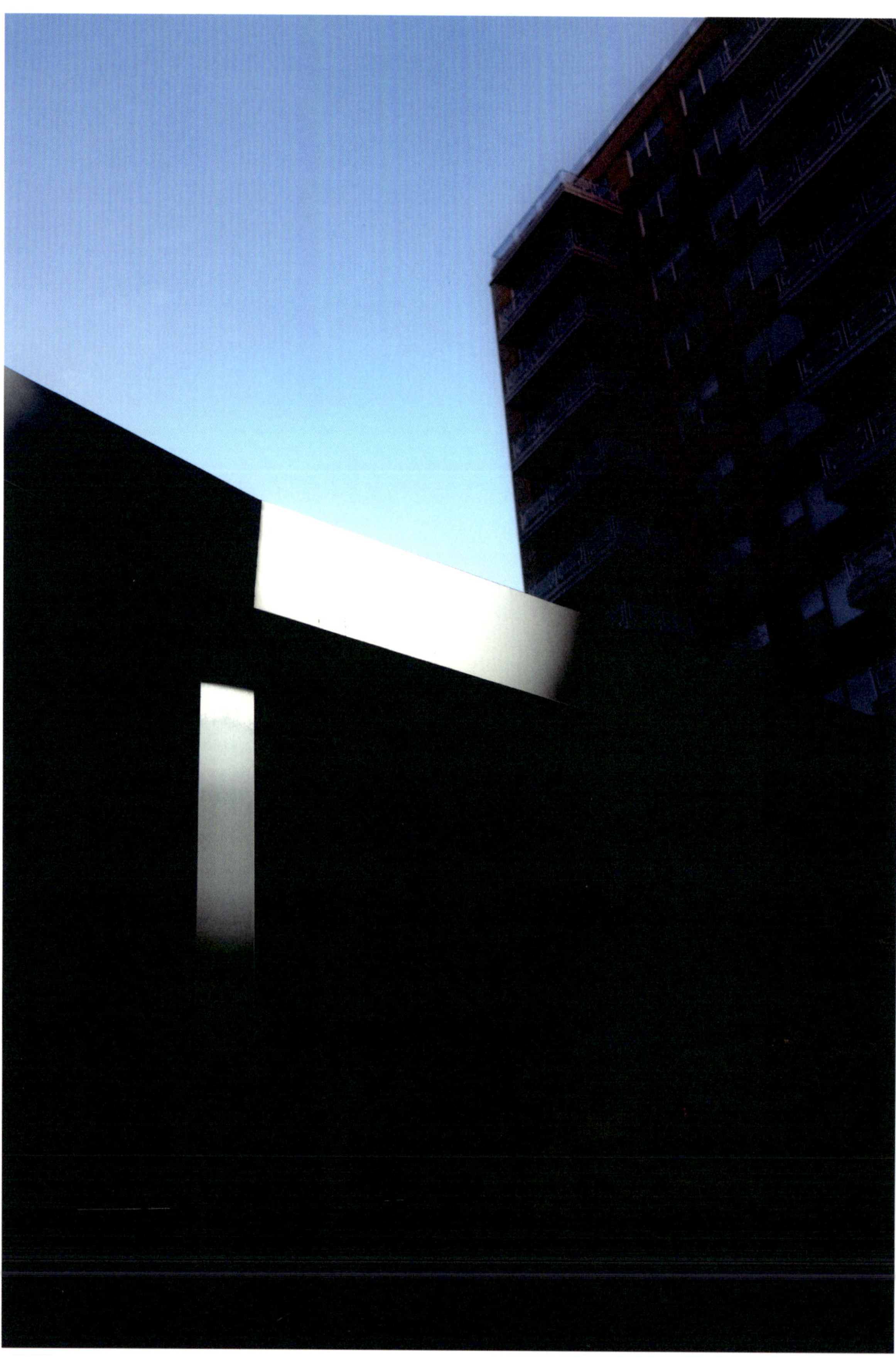

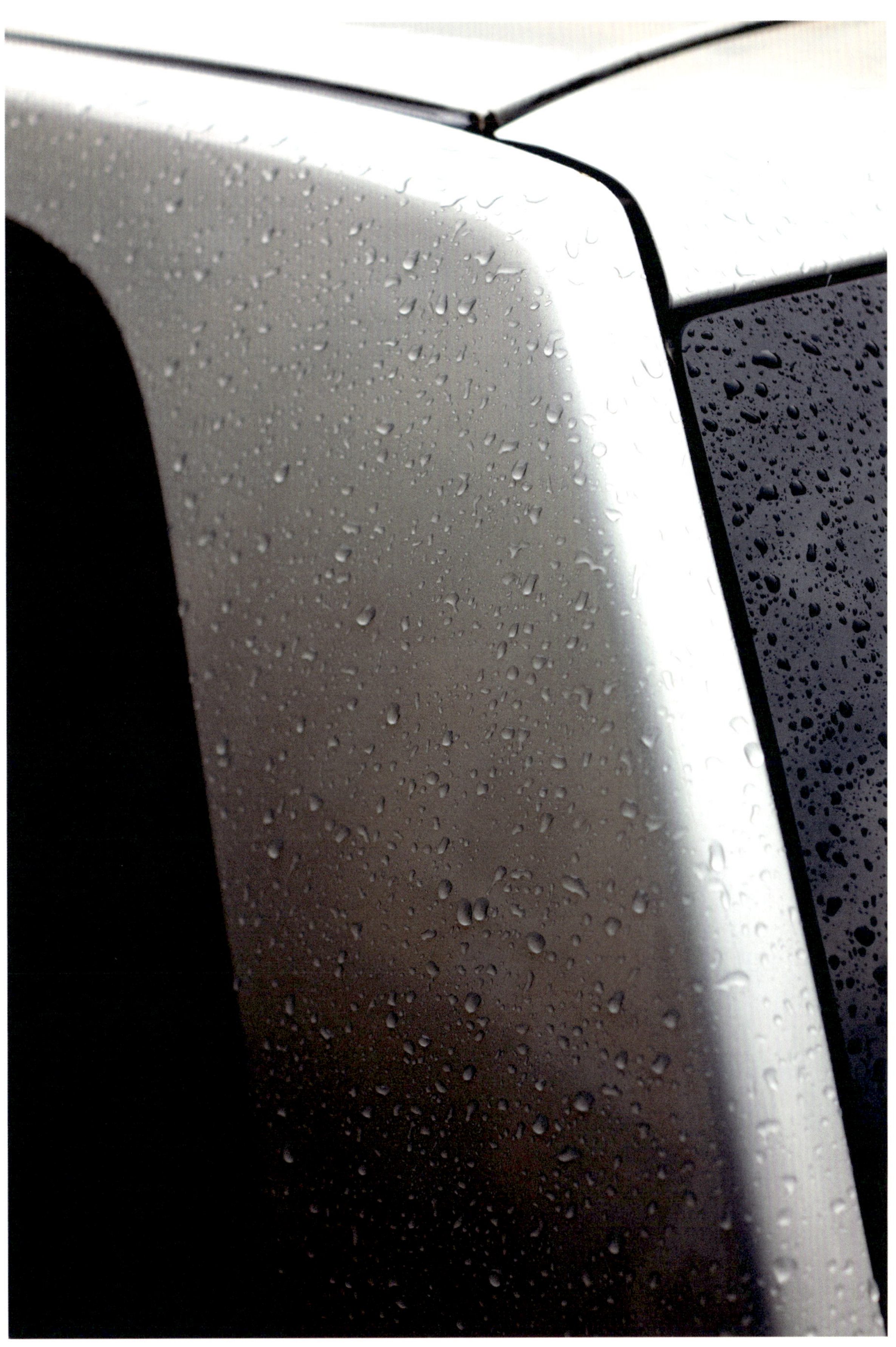

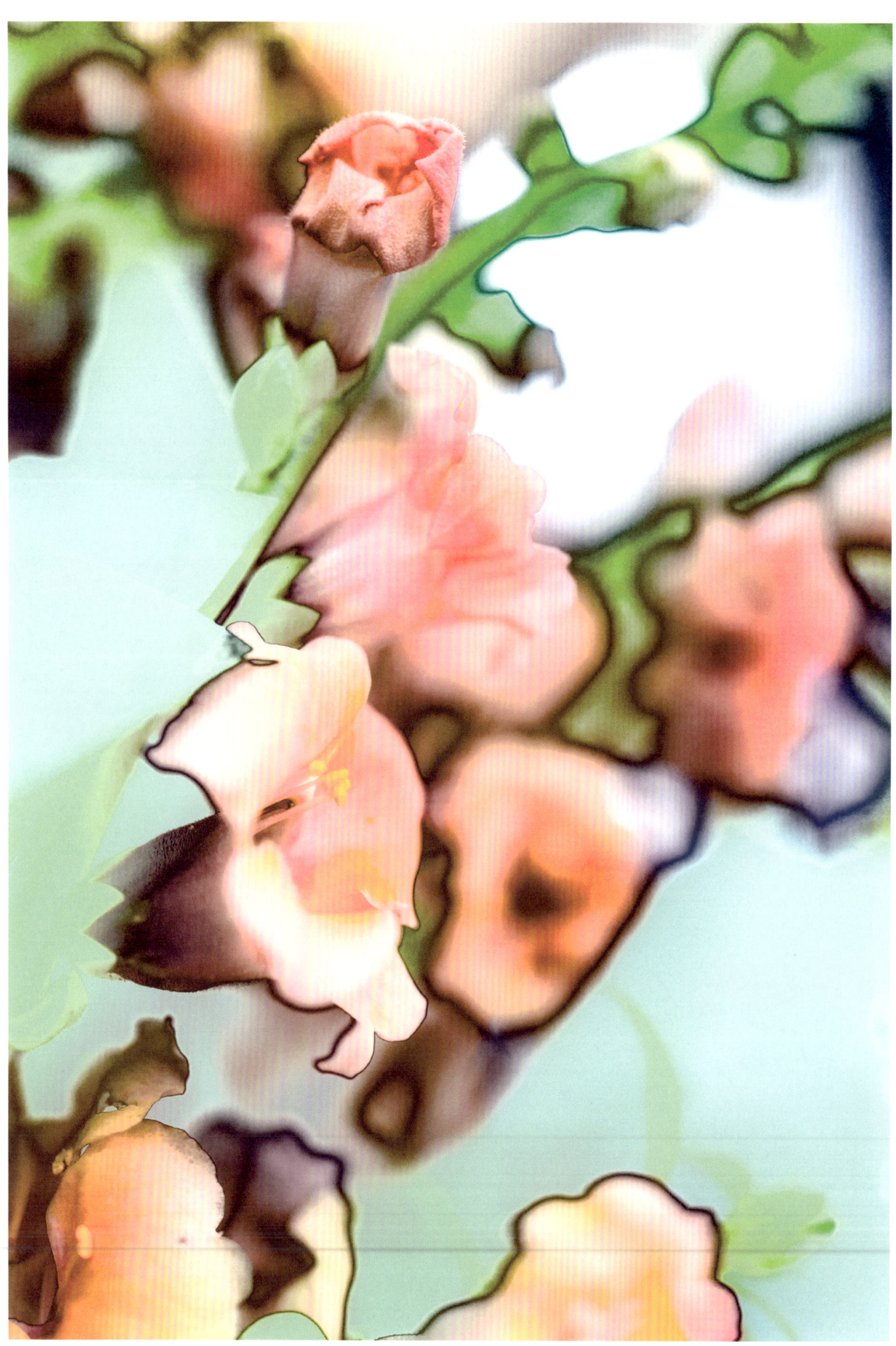

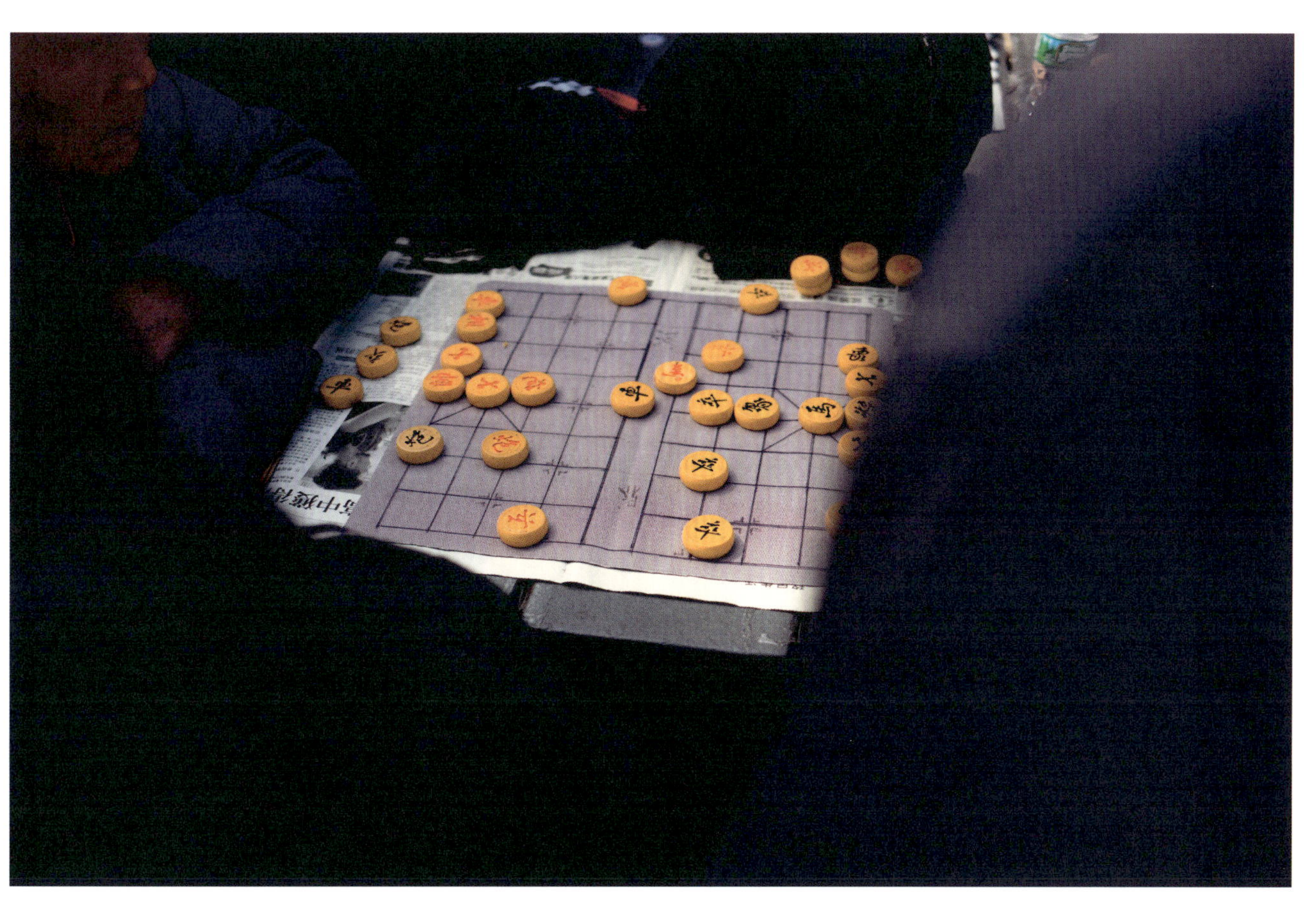

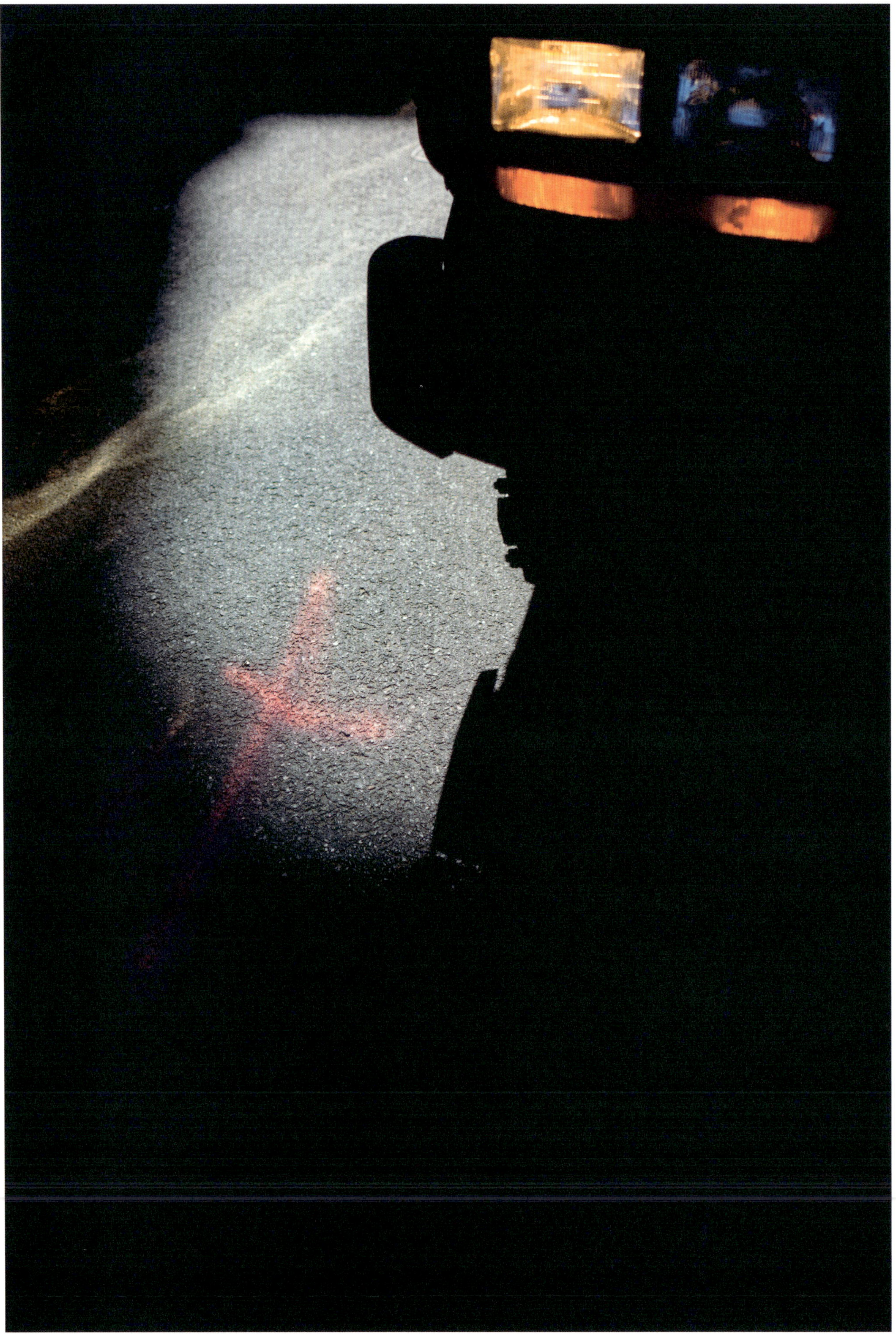

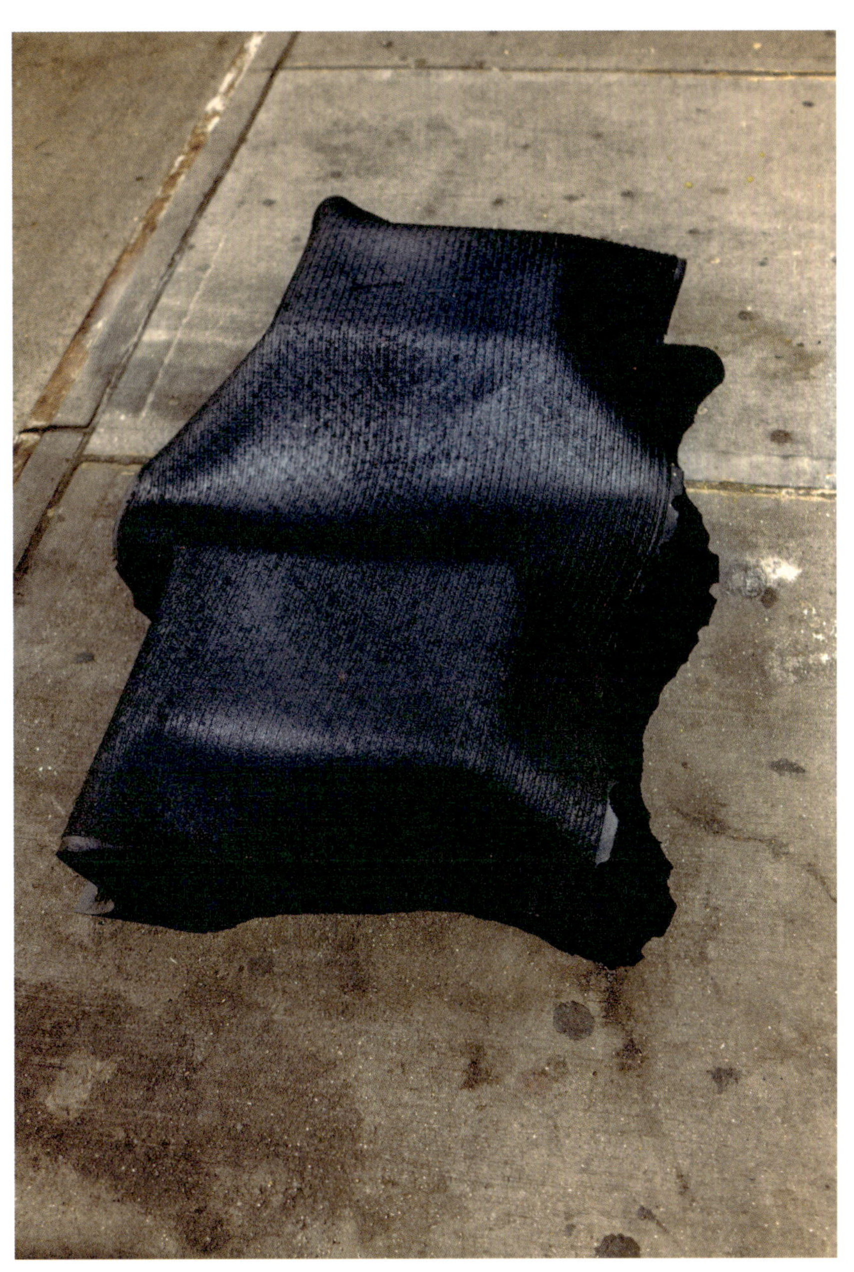

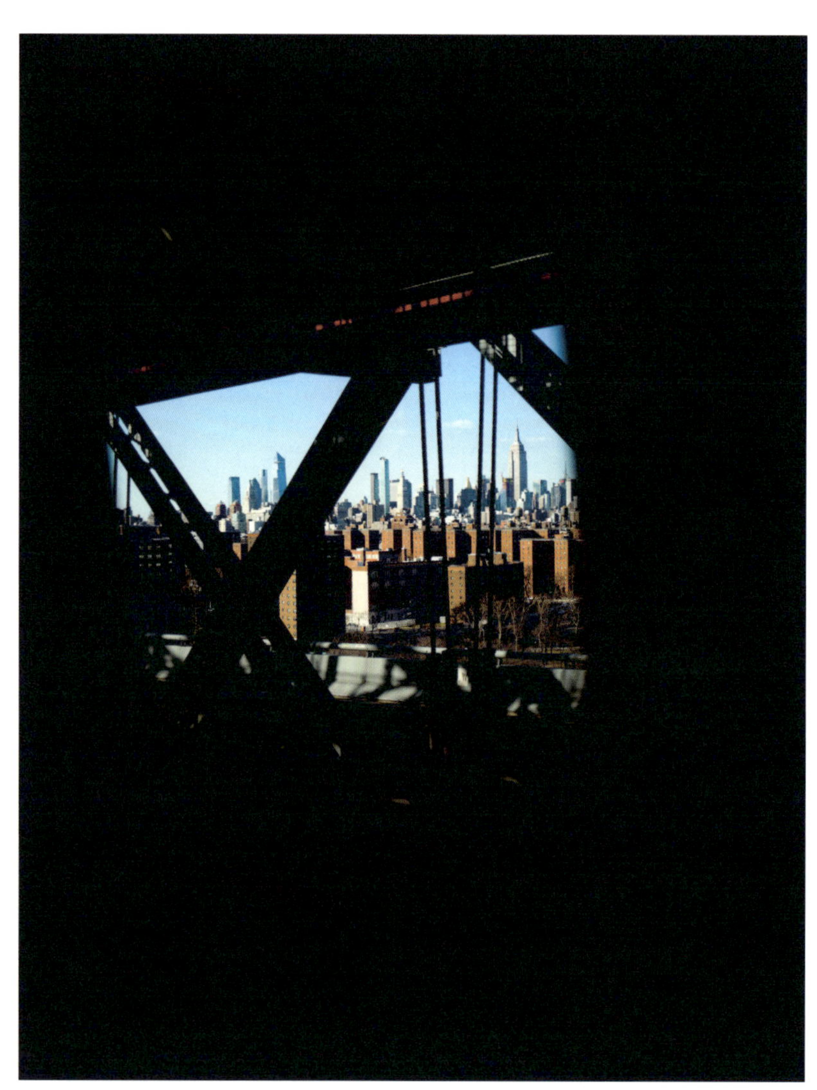

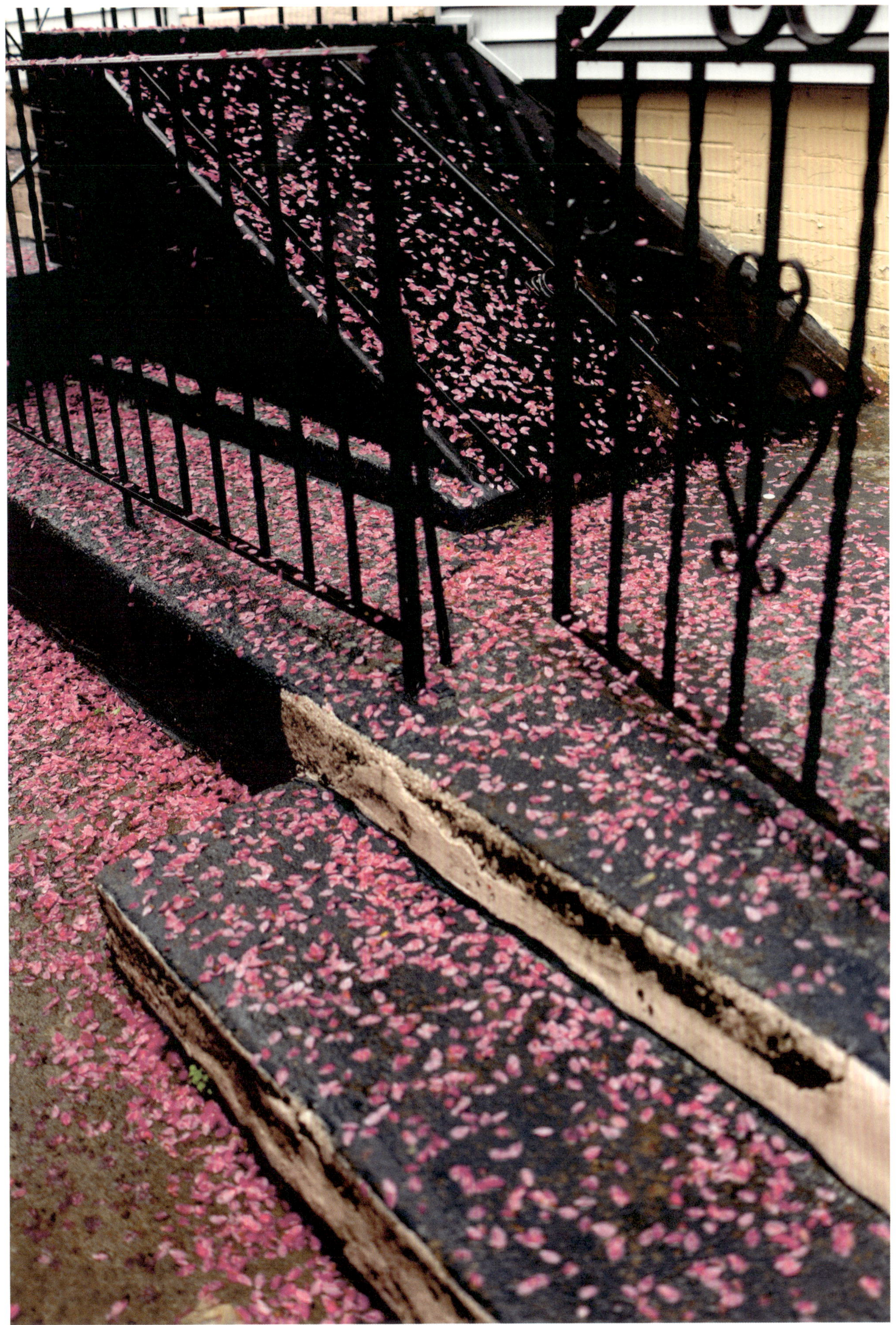

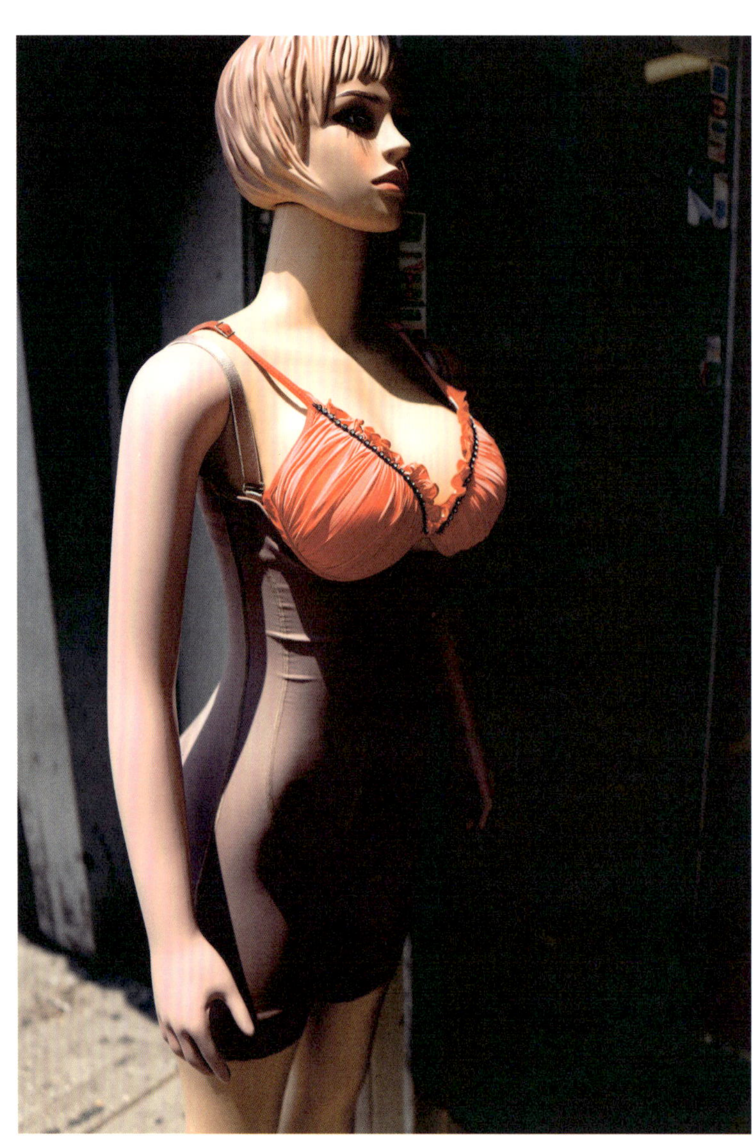

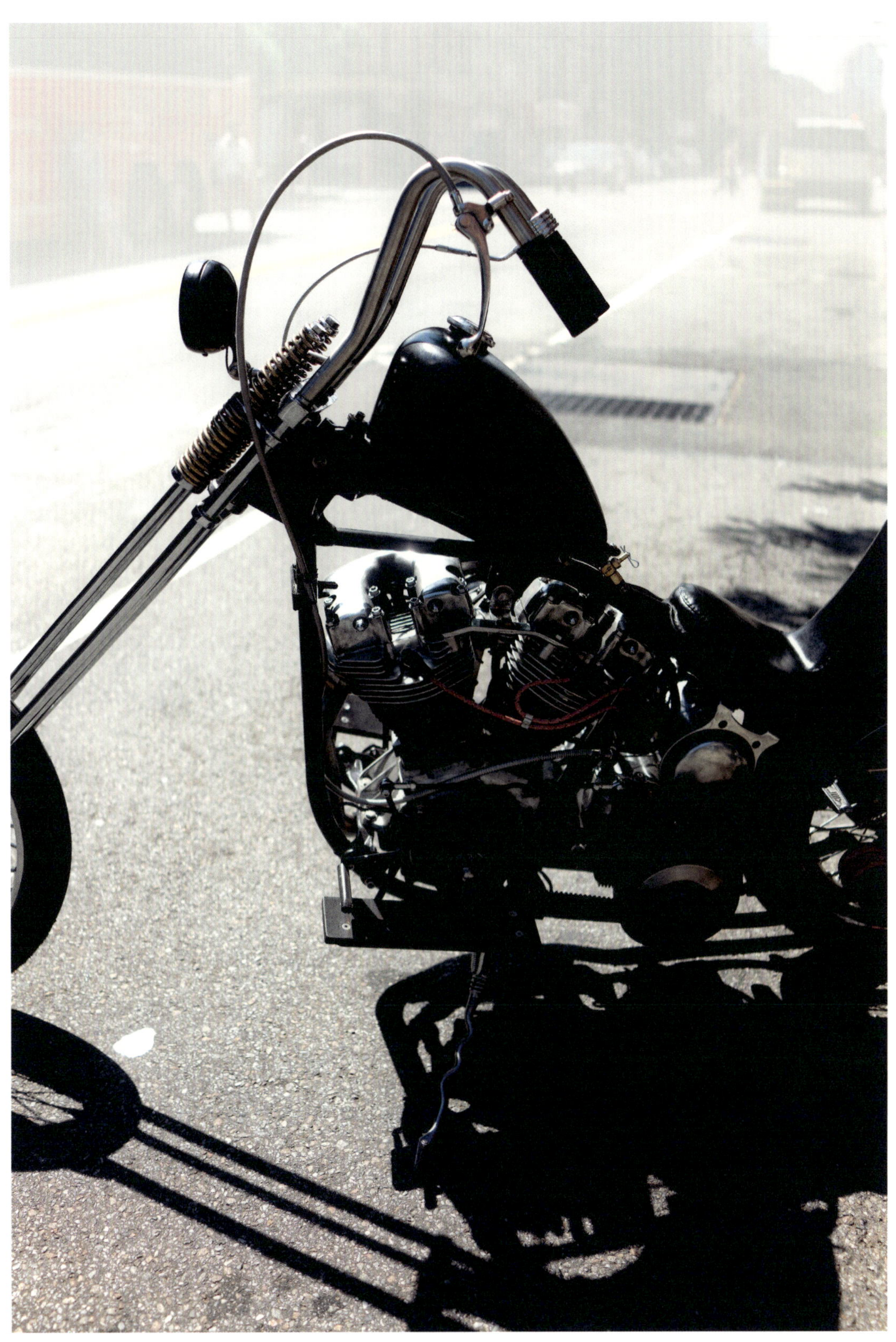

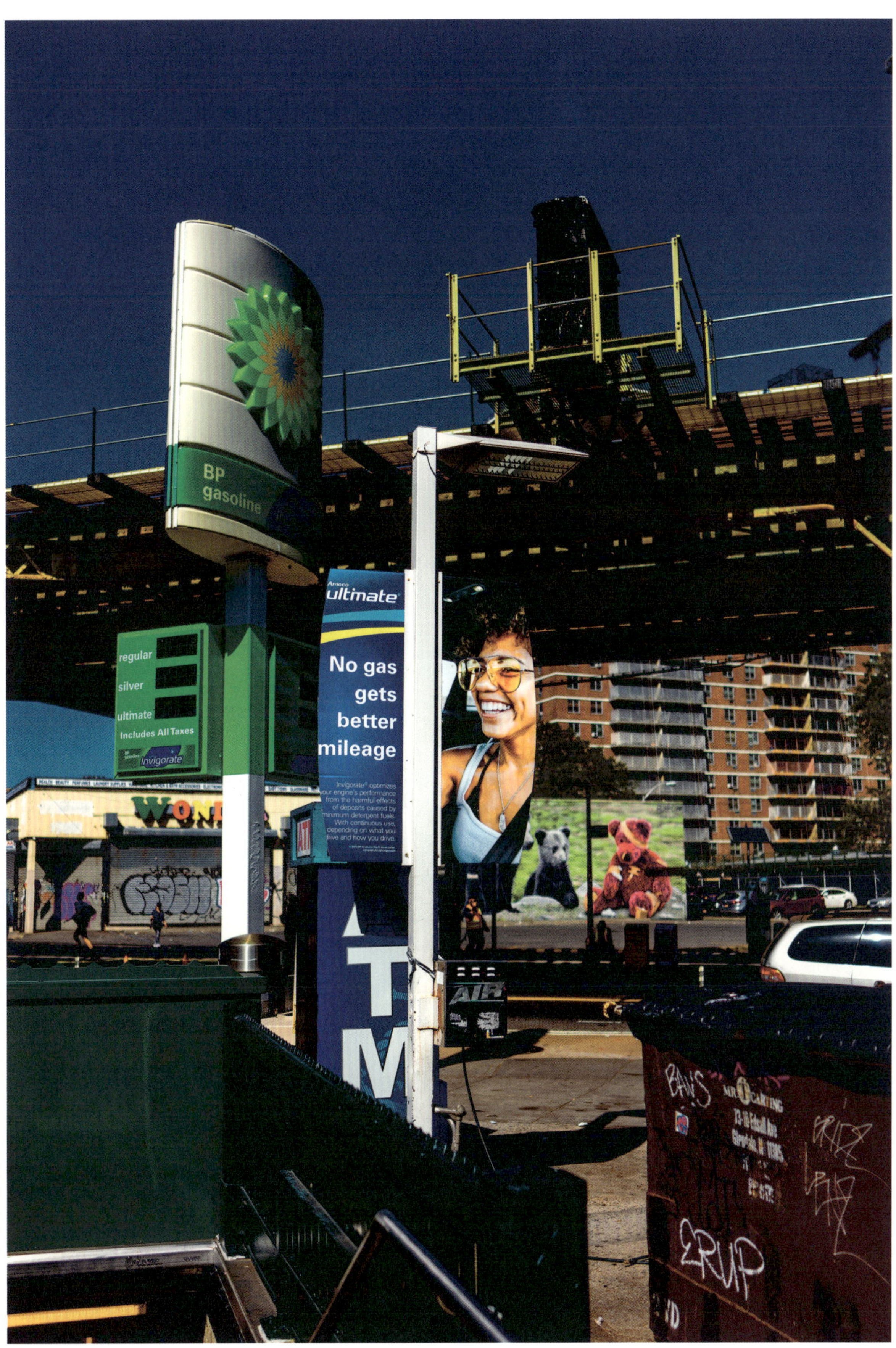
BP
gasoline
regular
silver
ultimate
Includes All Taxes
Invigorate
Amoco
ultimate
No gas
gets
better
mileage
ATM
AIR
2RUP

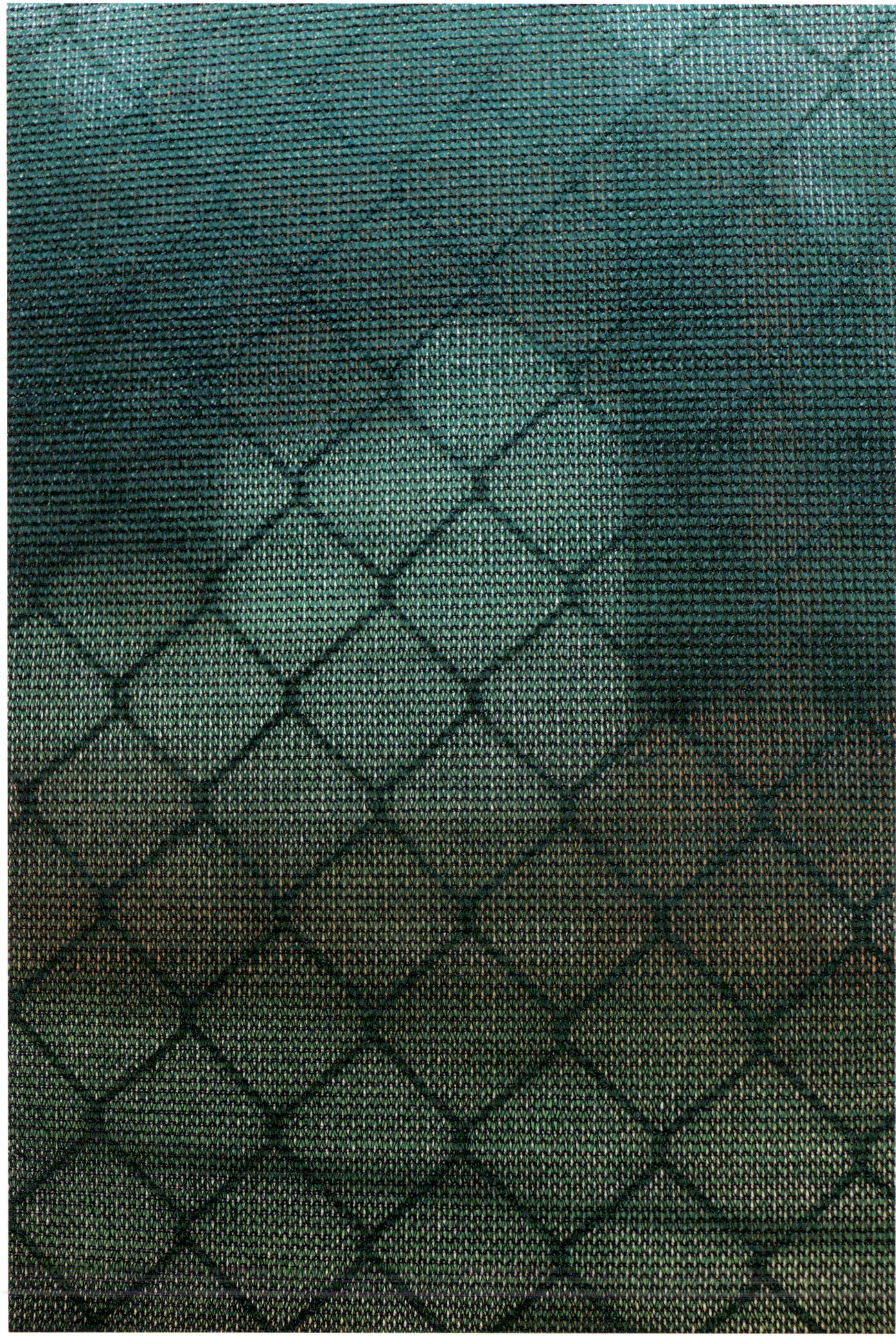

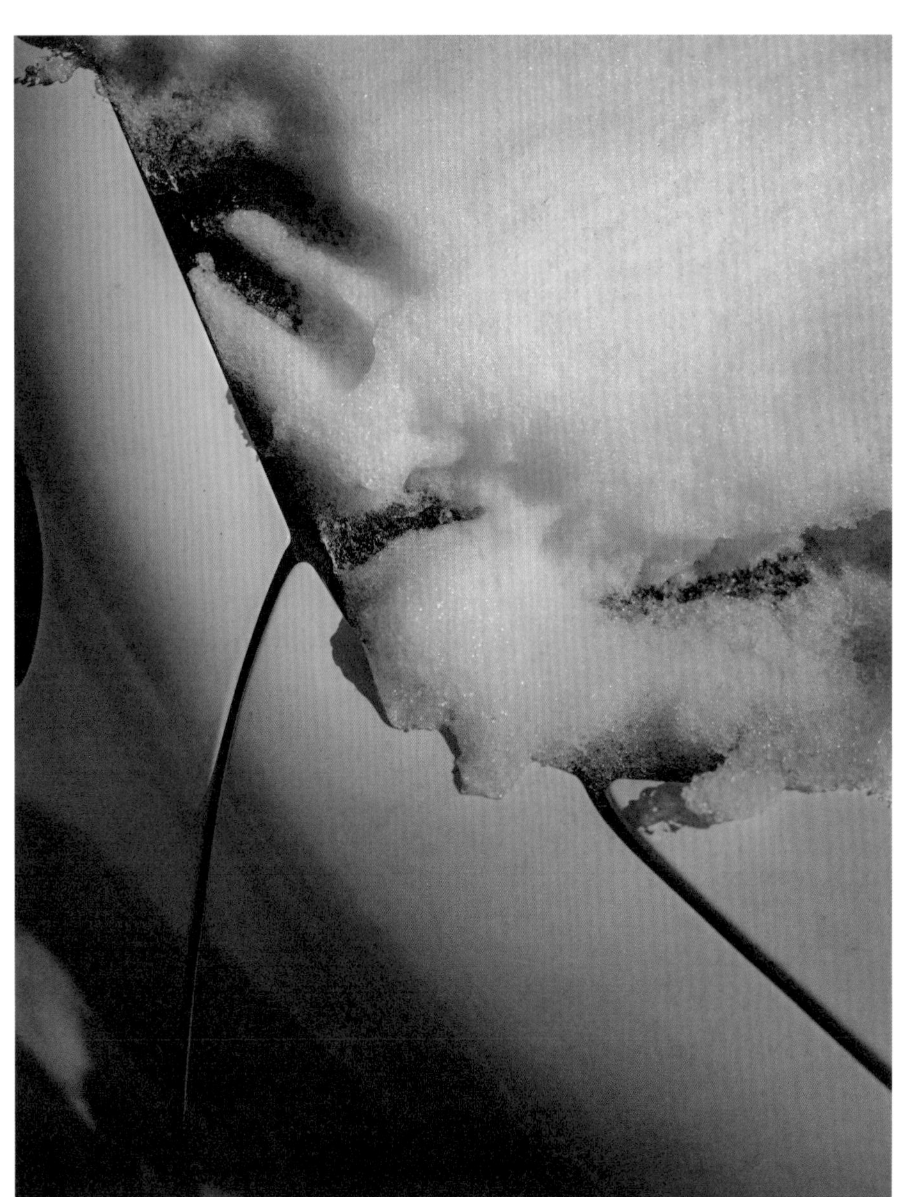

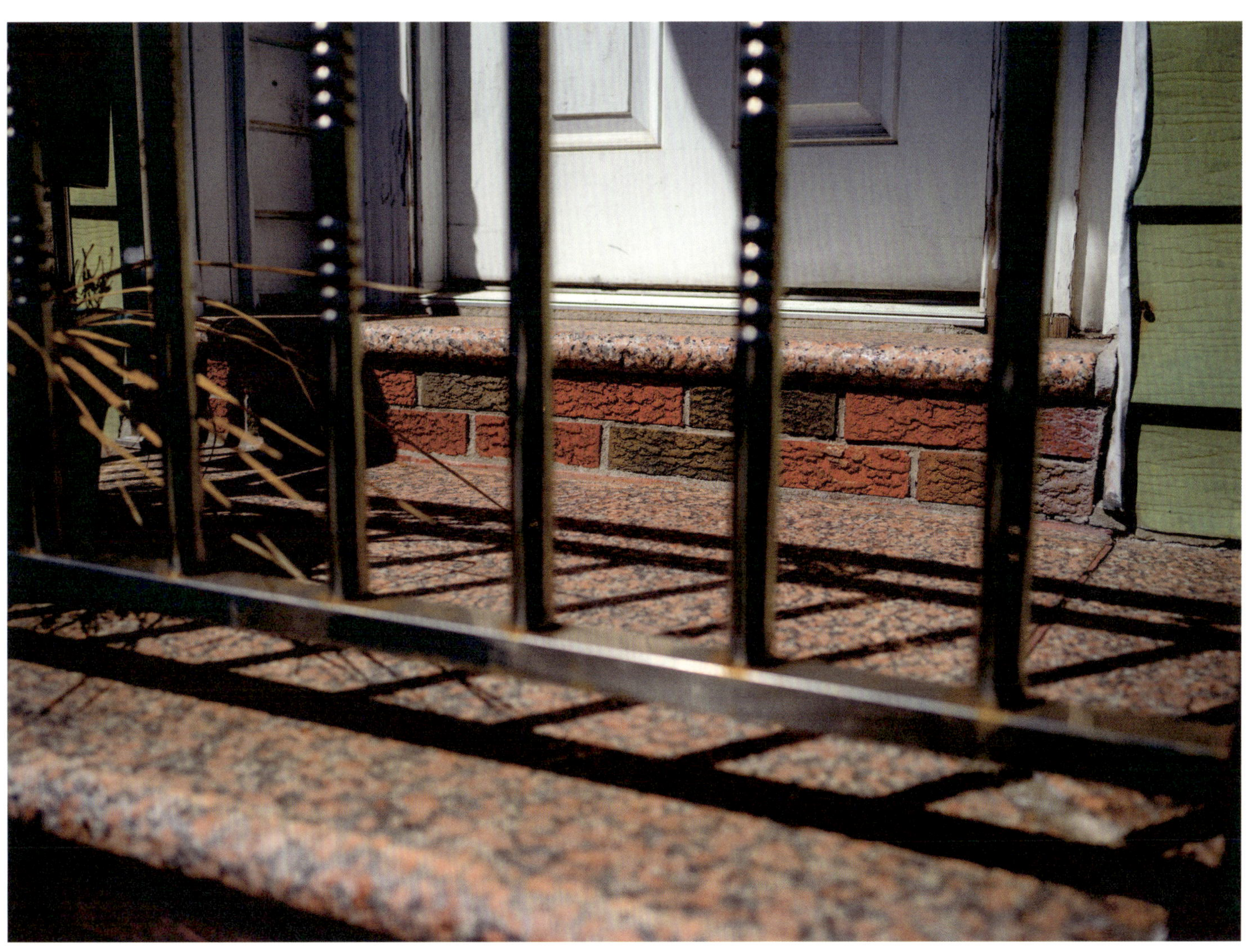

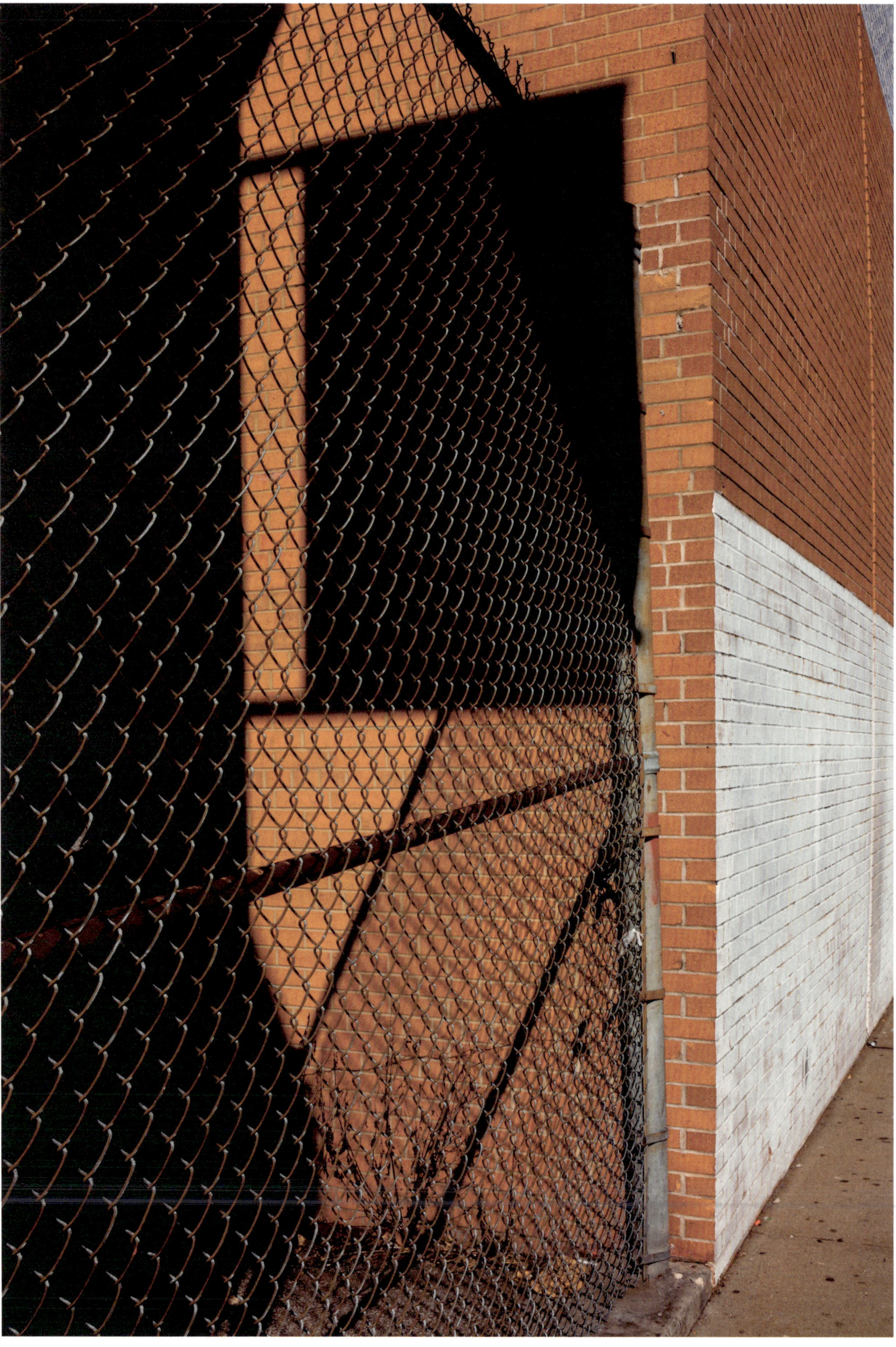

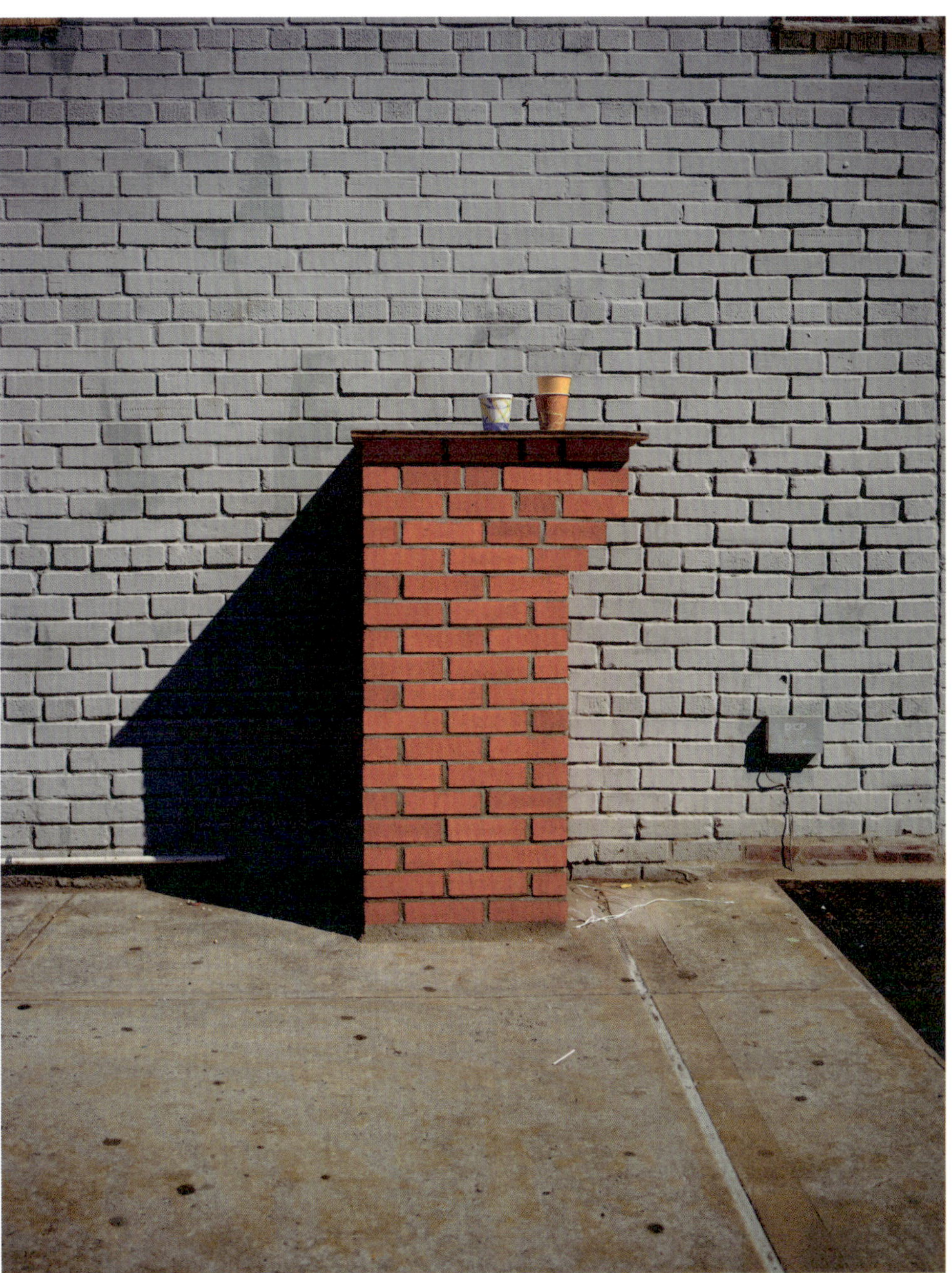

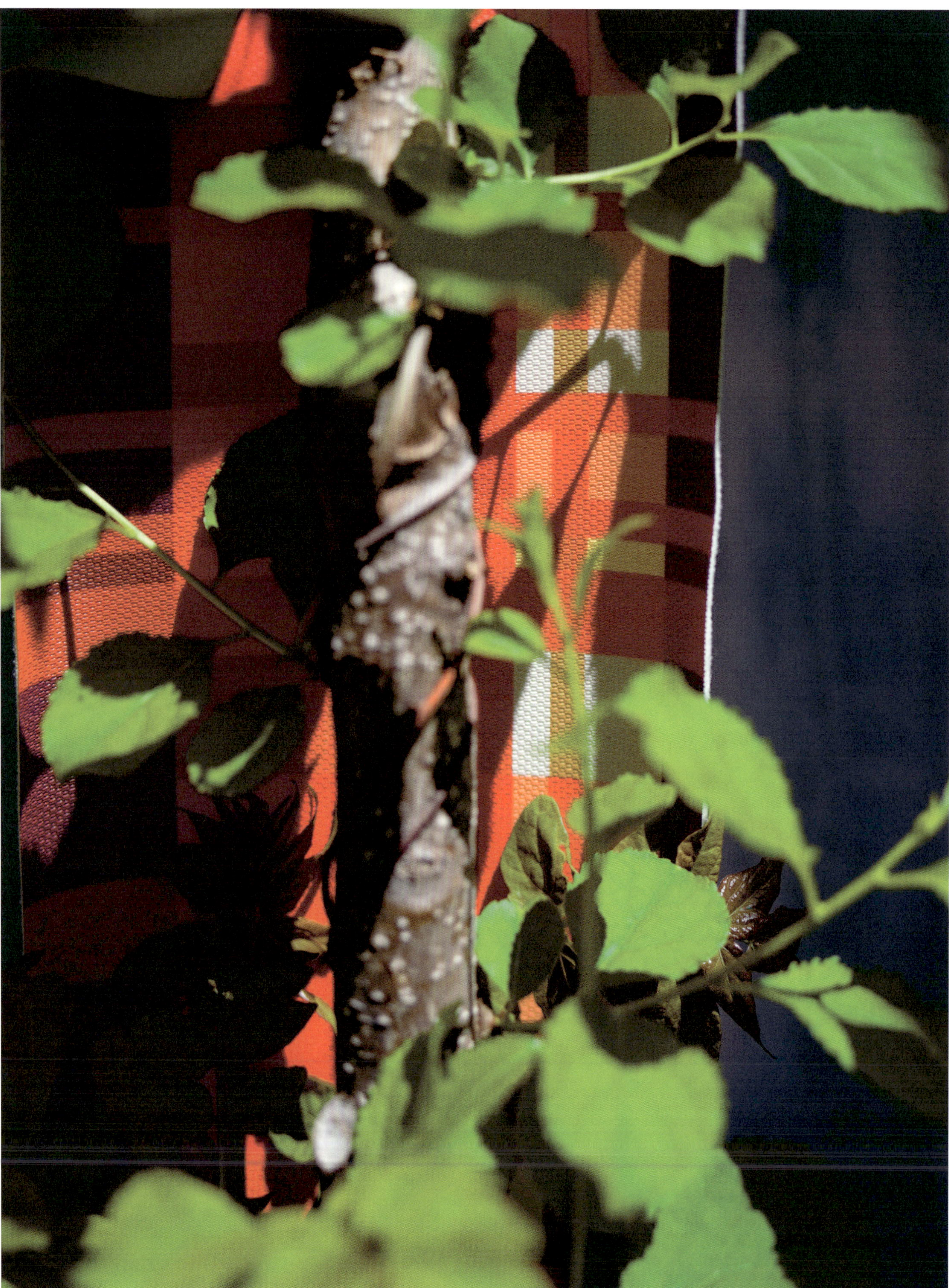

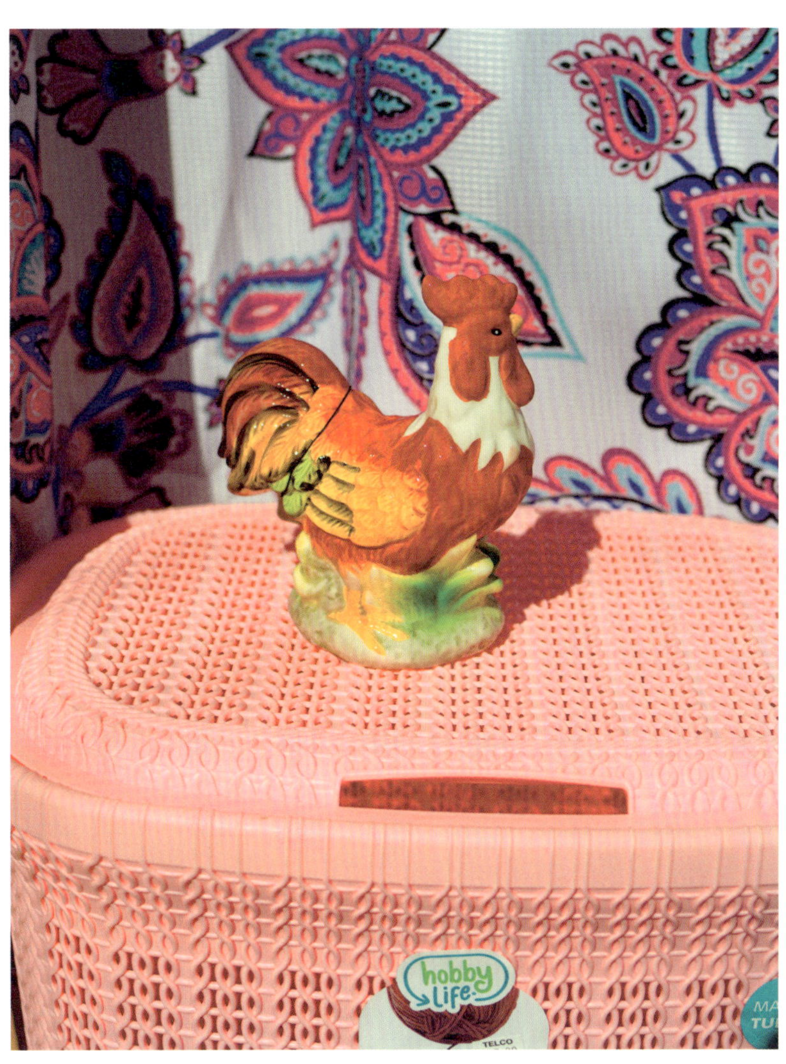
hobby
life.
TELCO

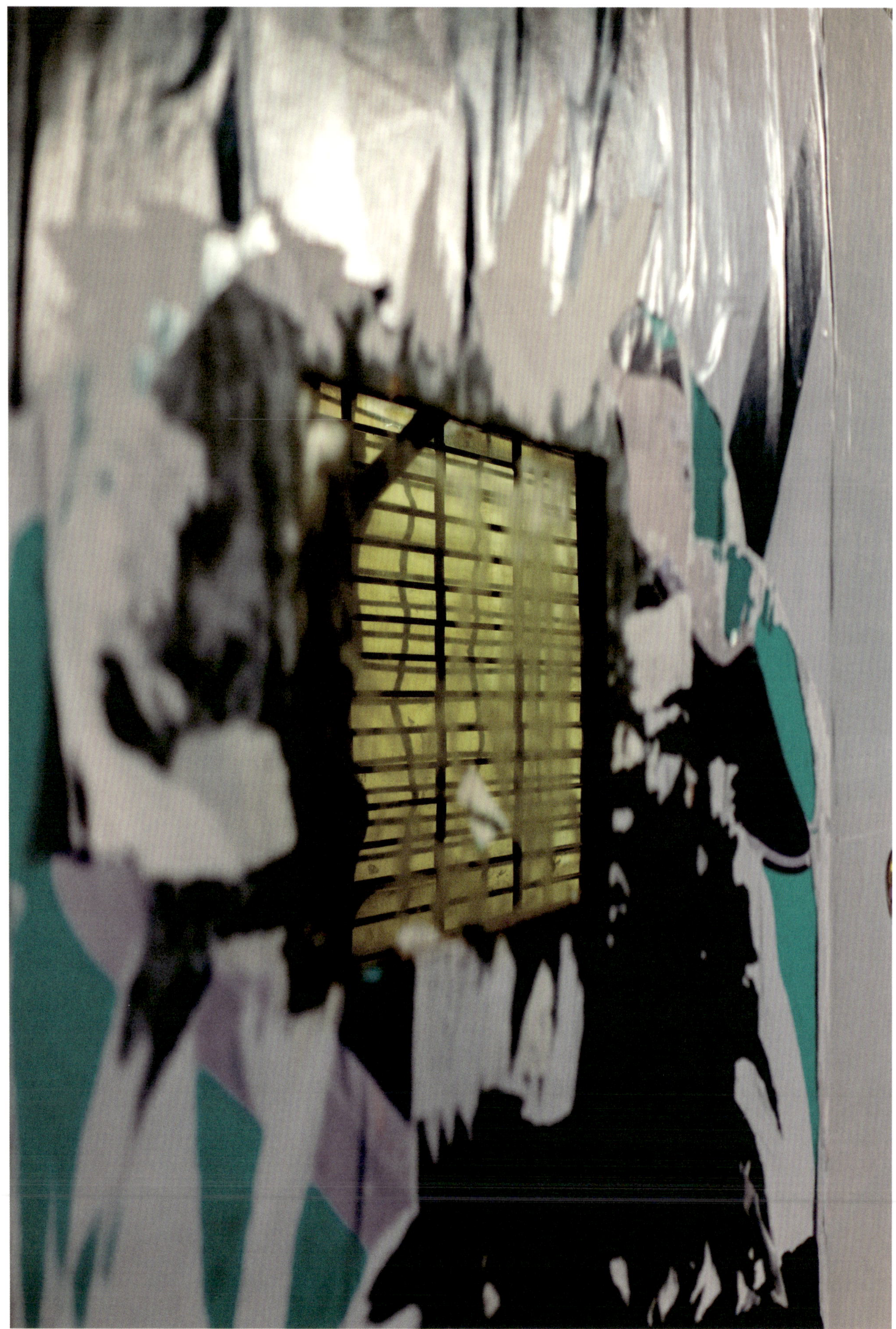

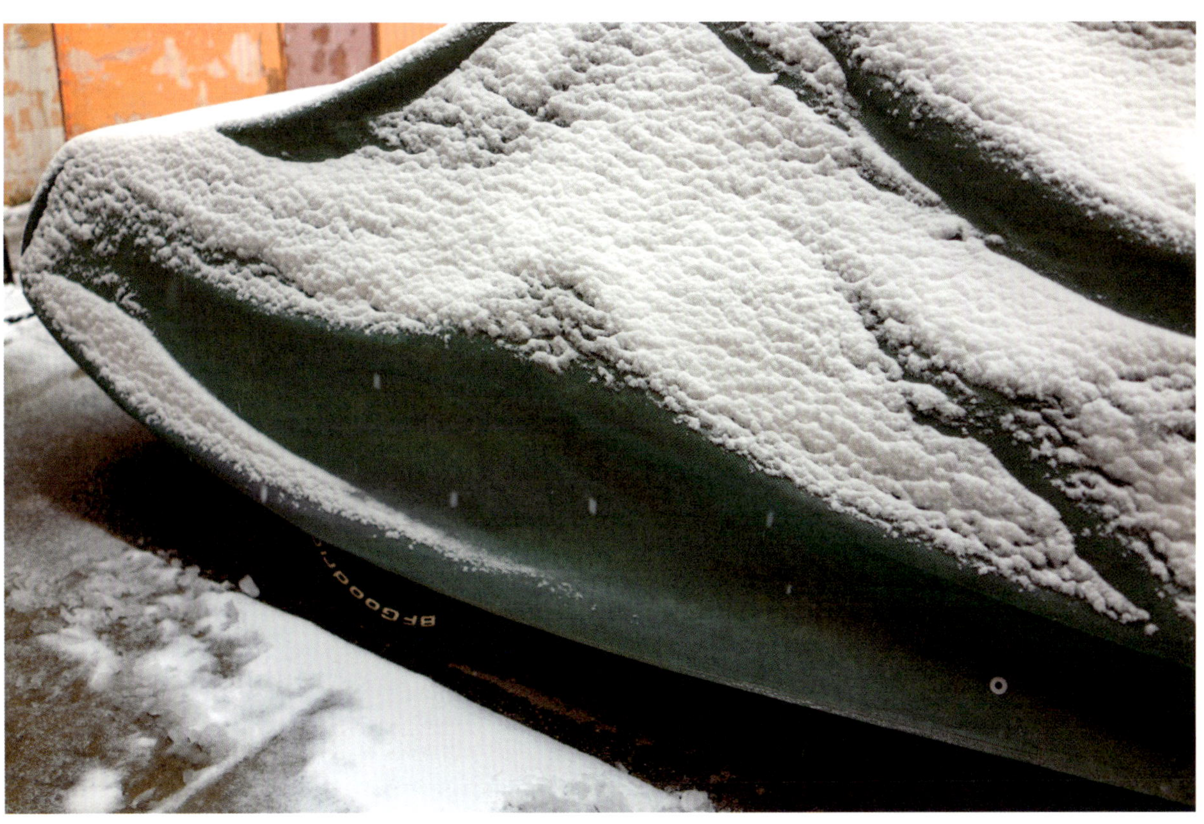

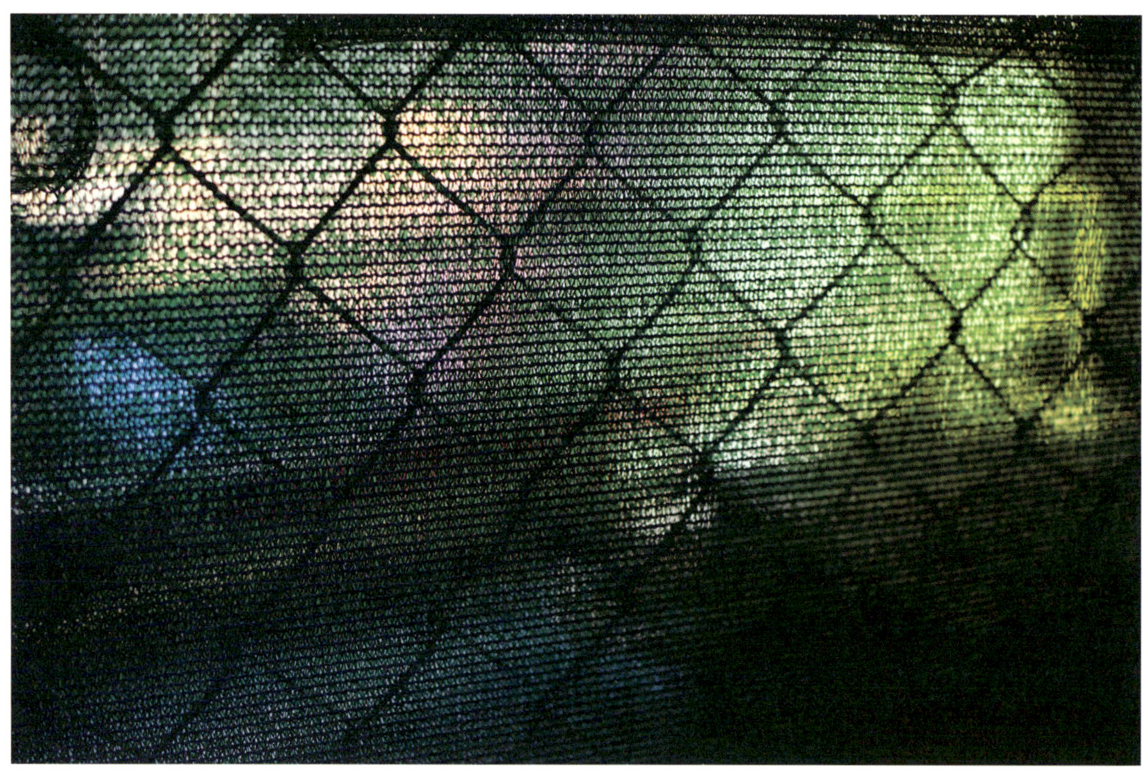

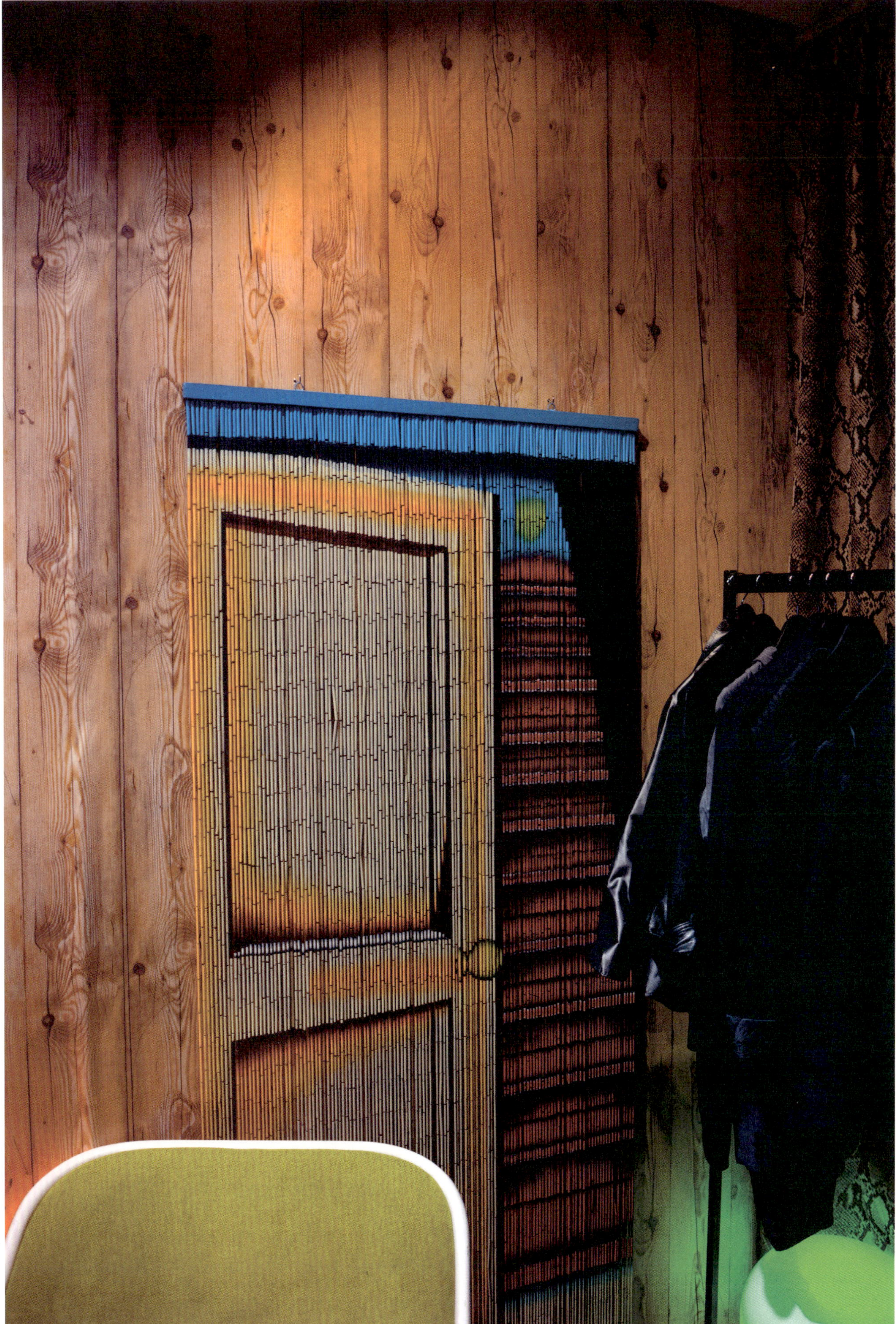

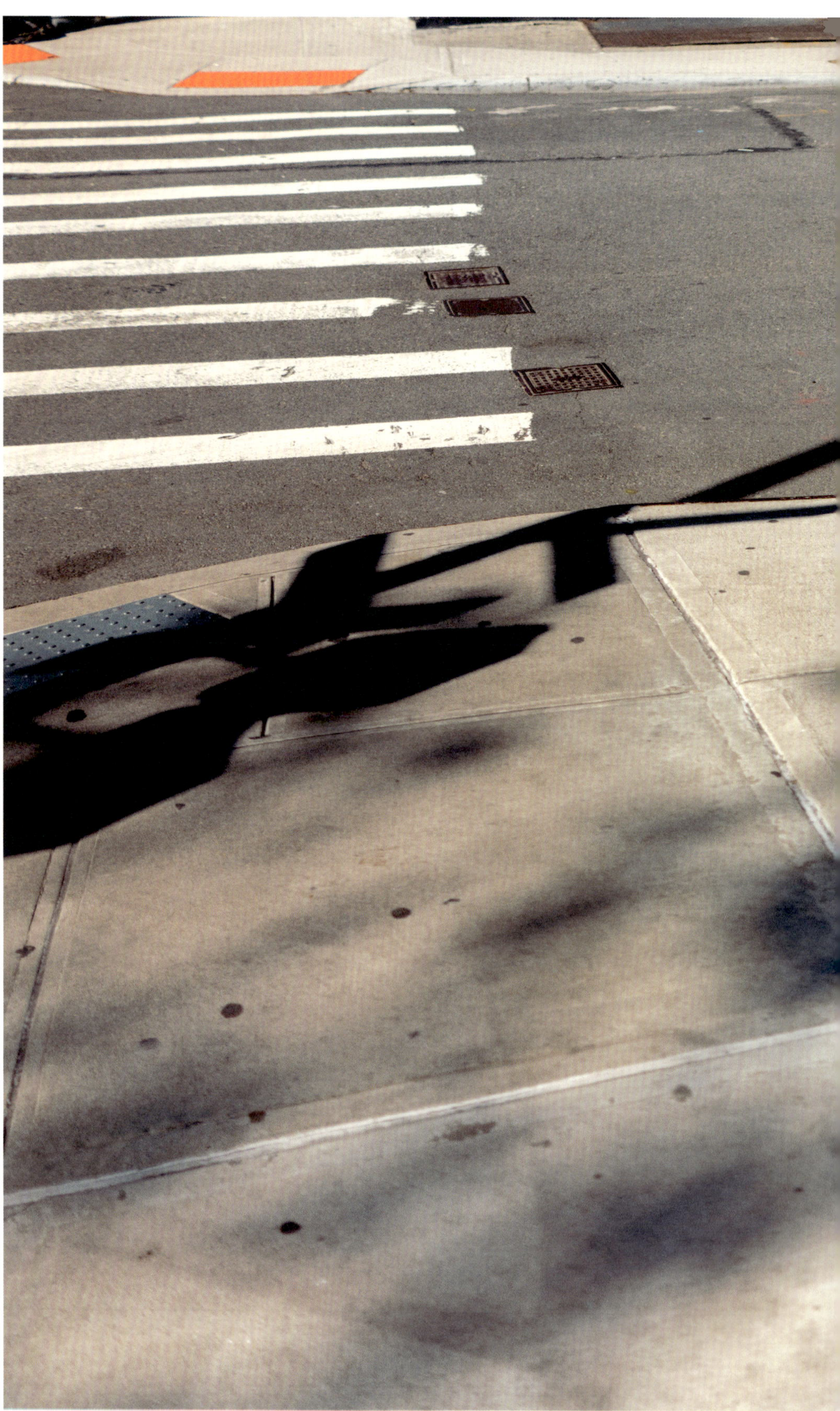

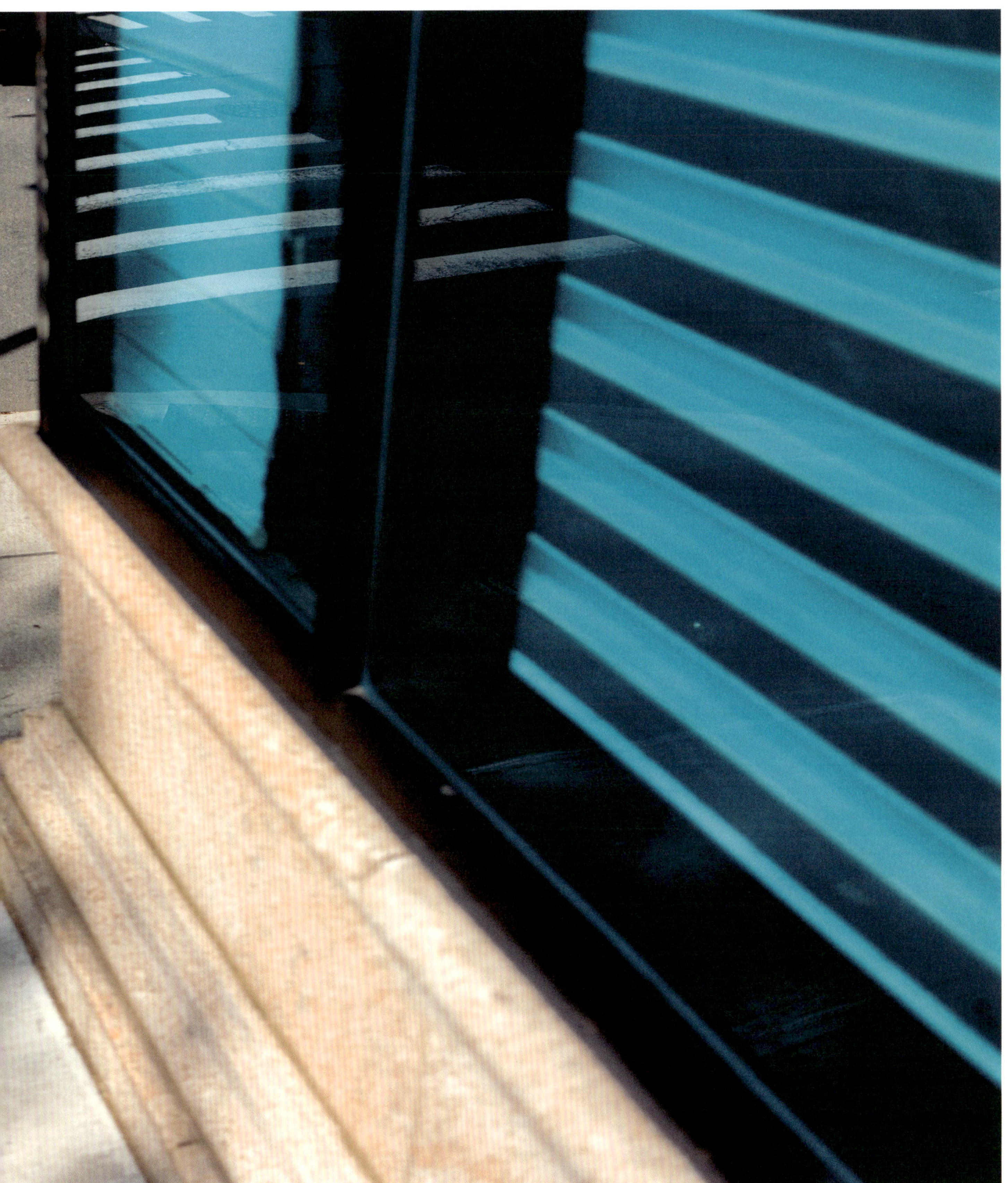

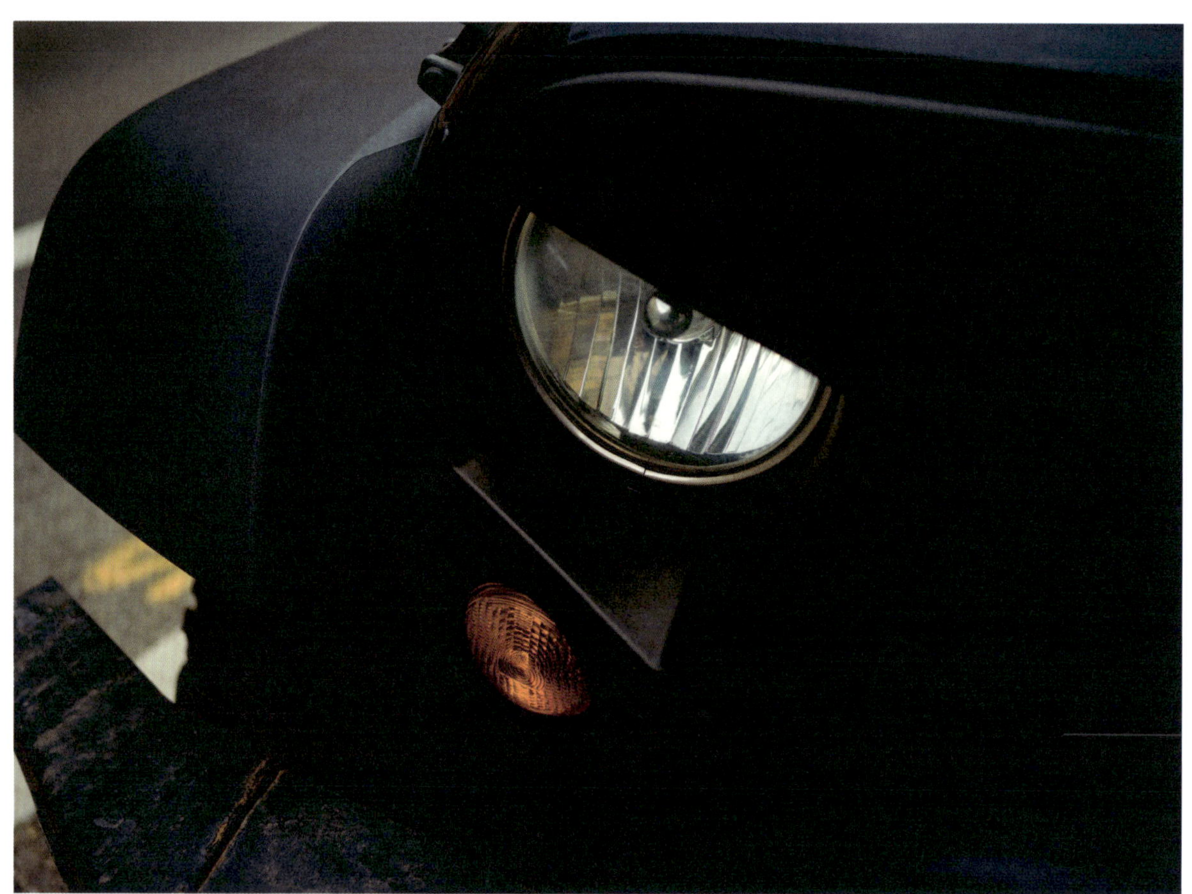

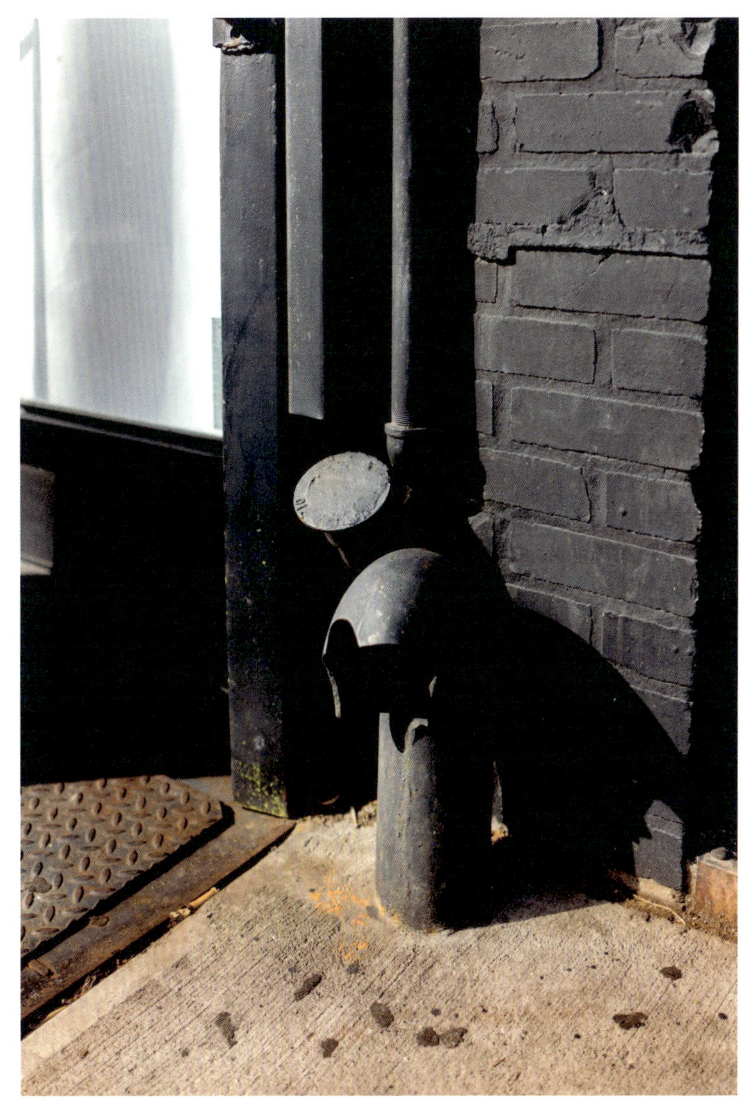

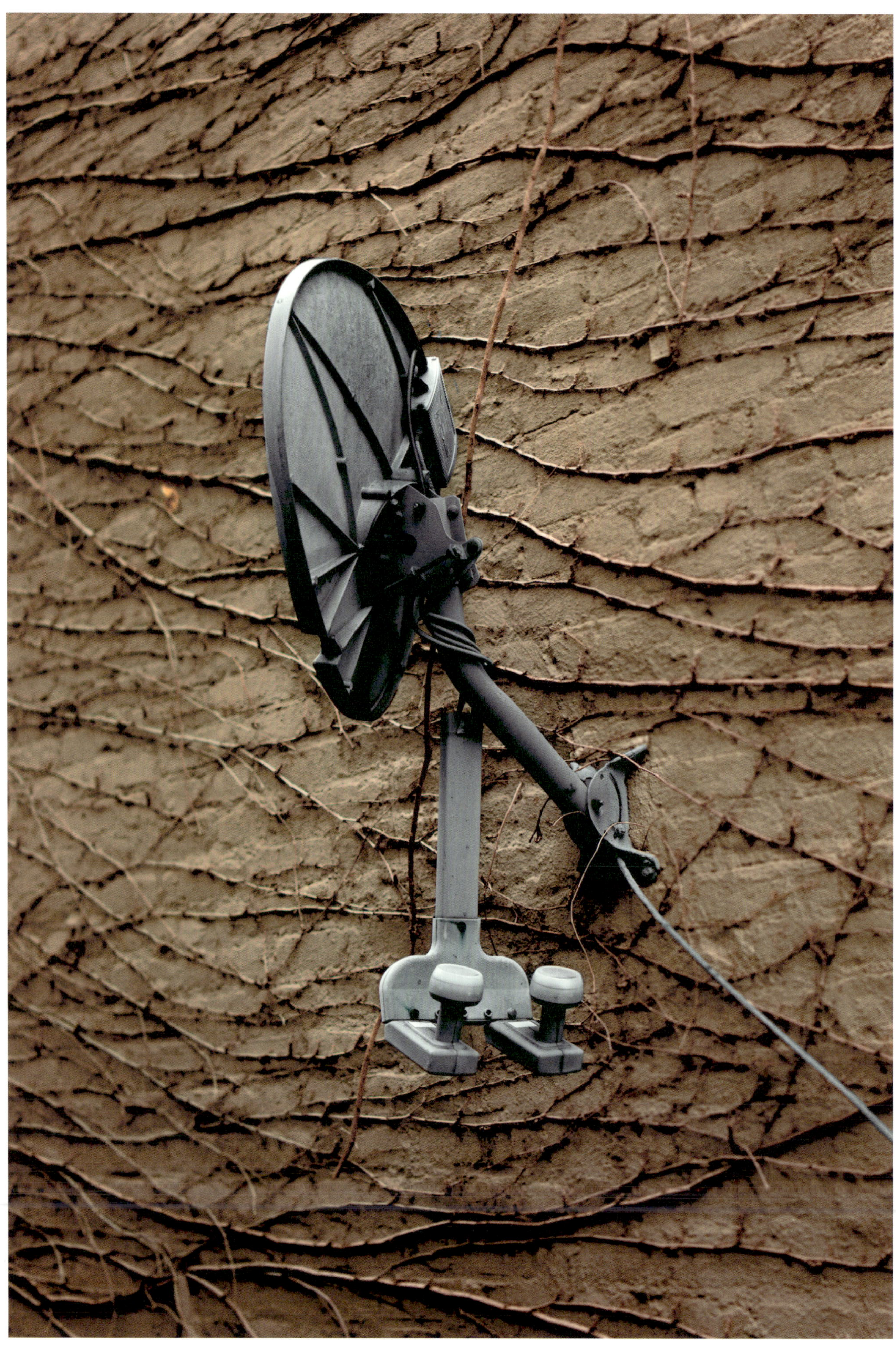

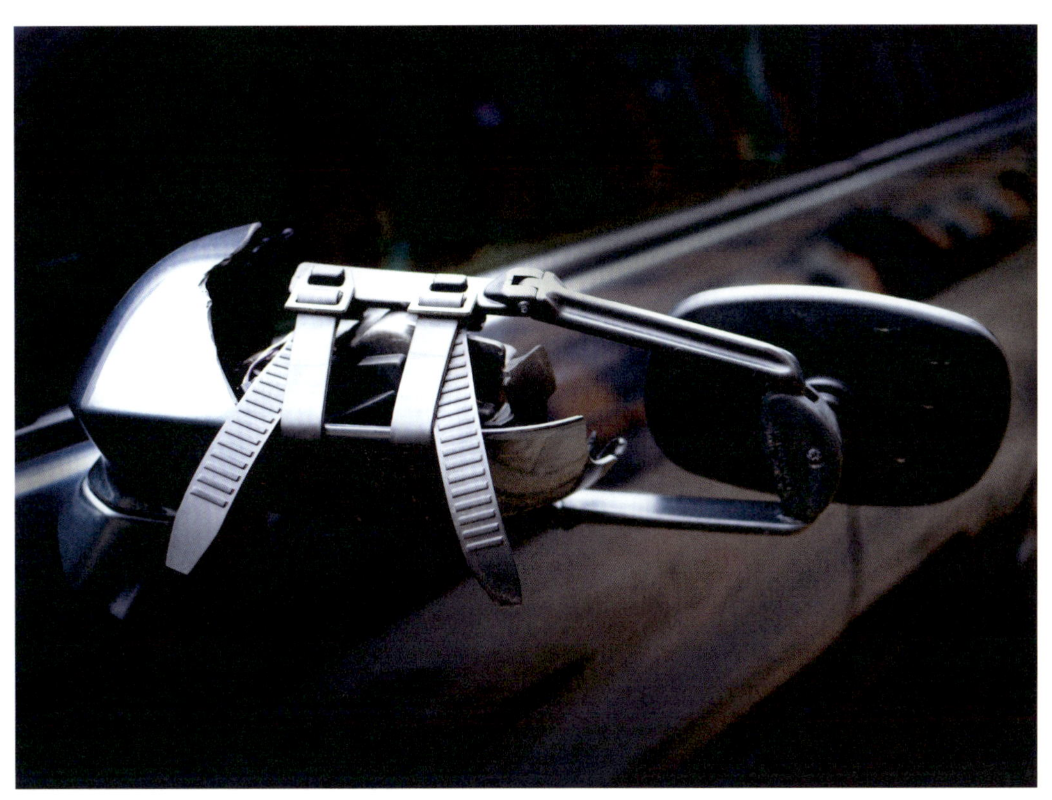

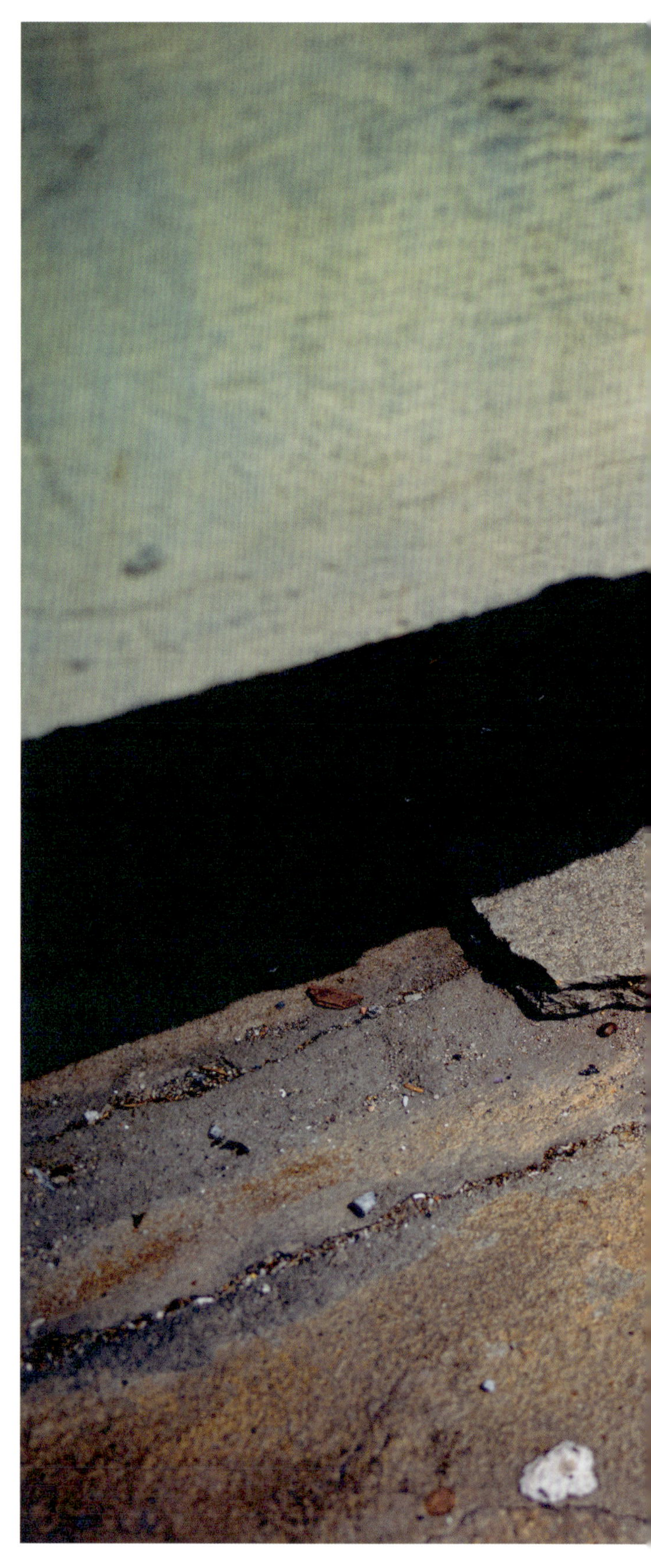

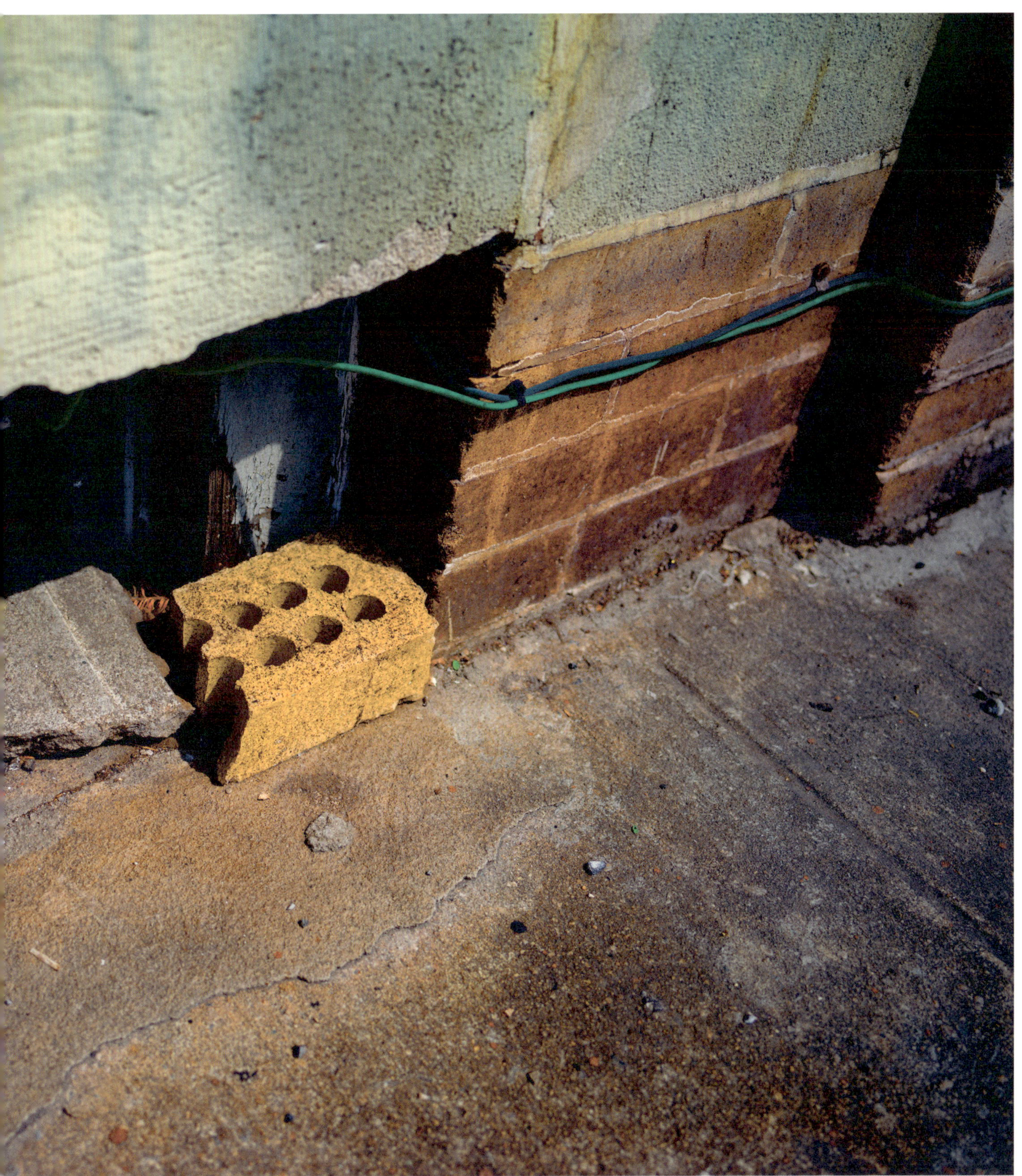

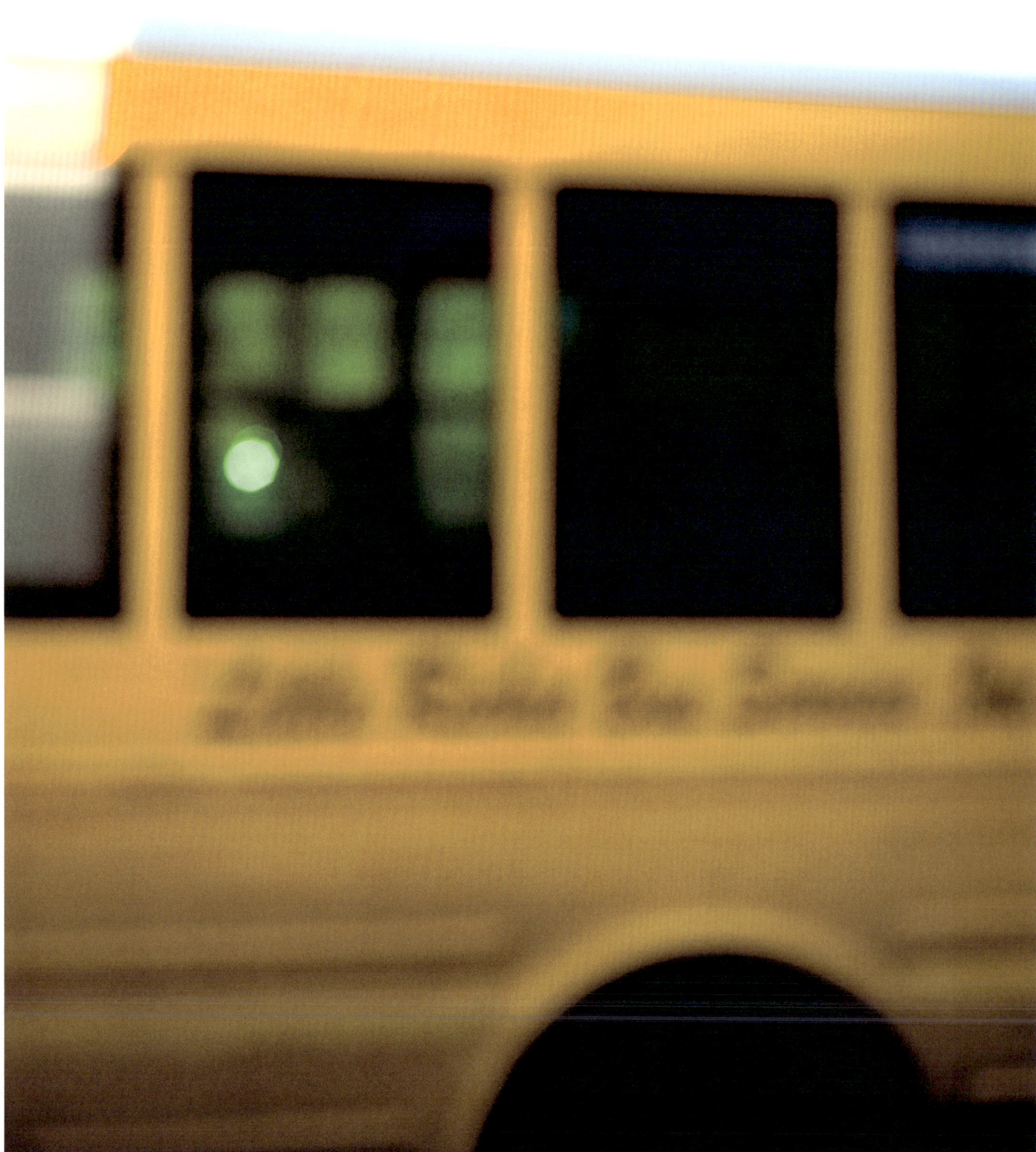

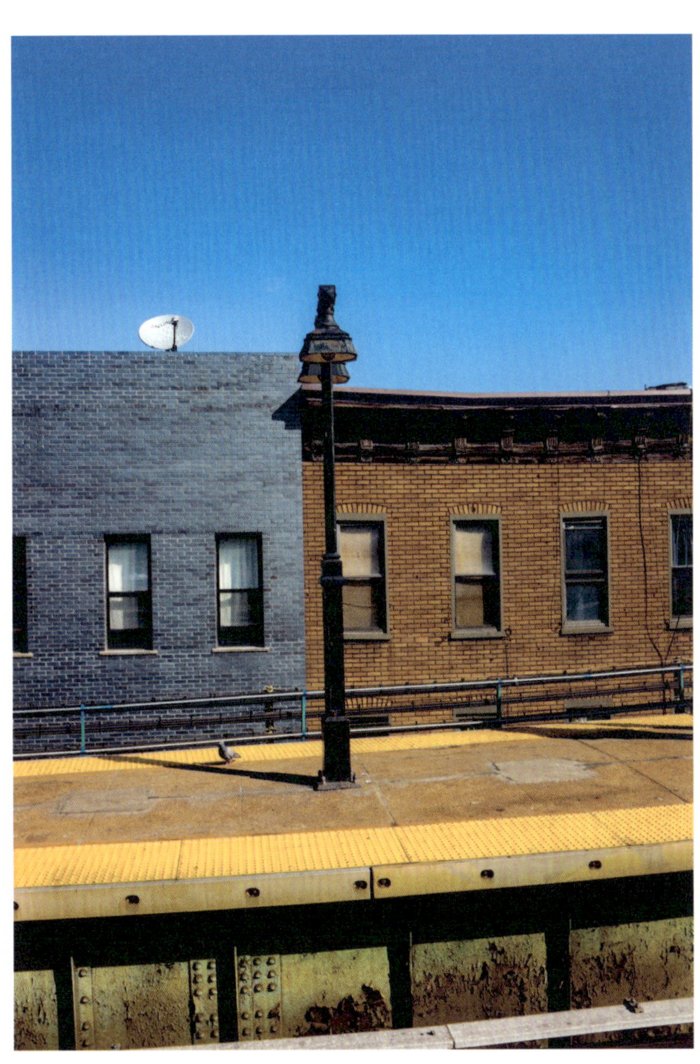

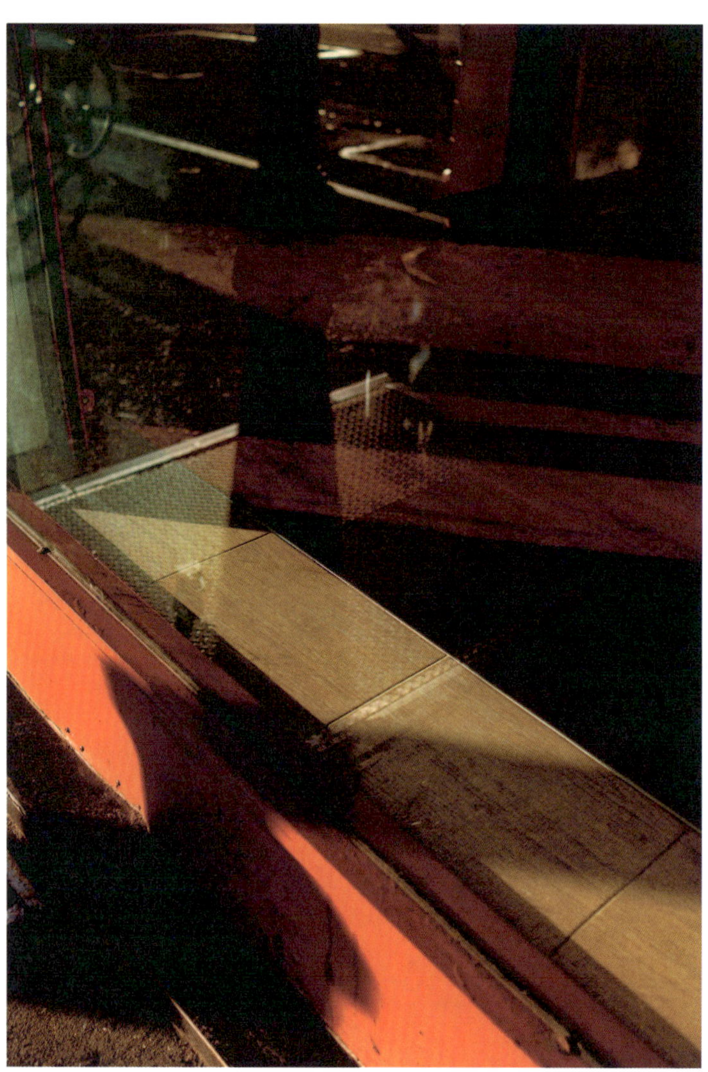

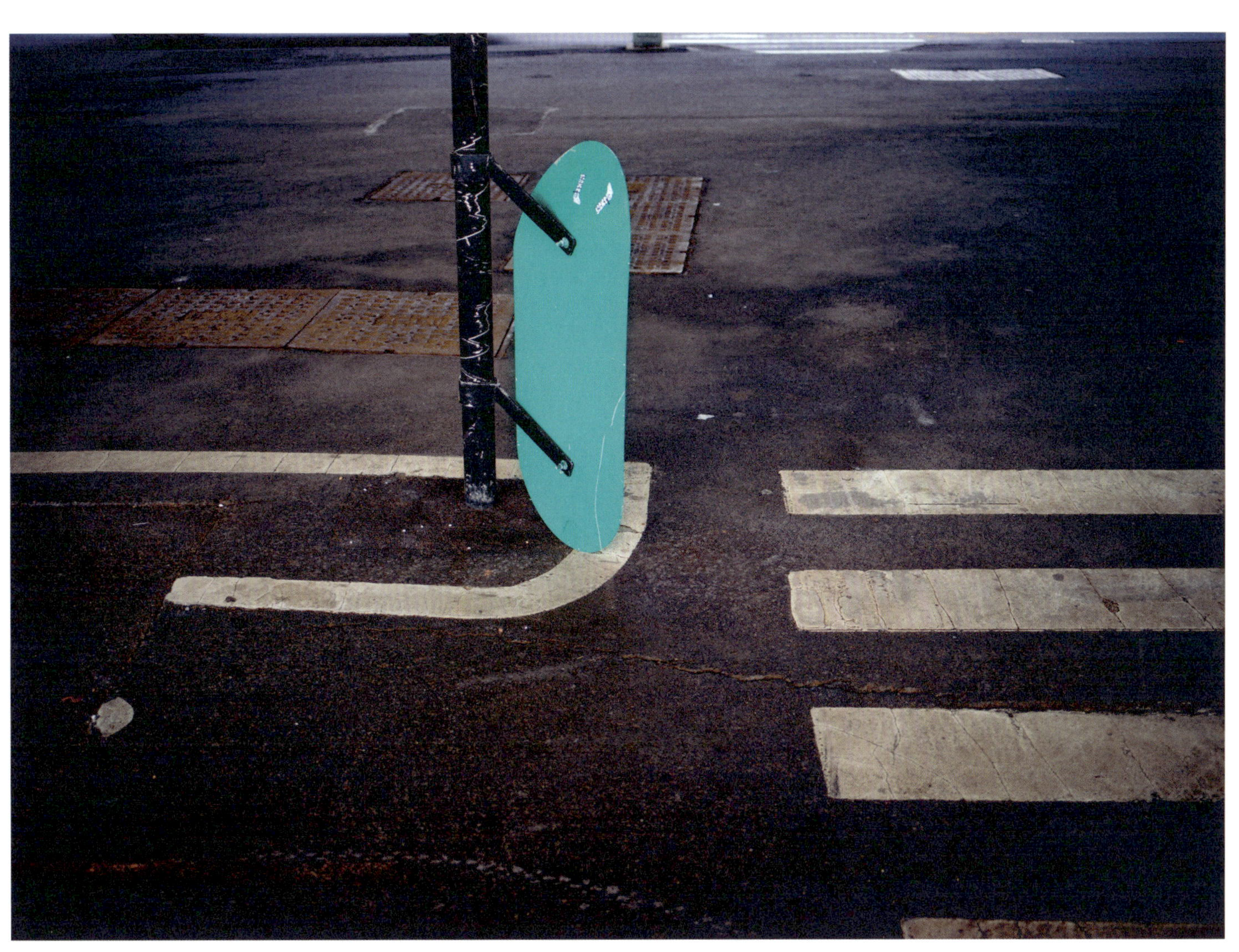

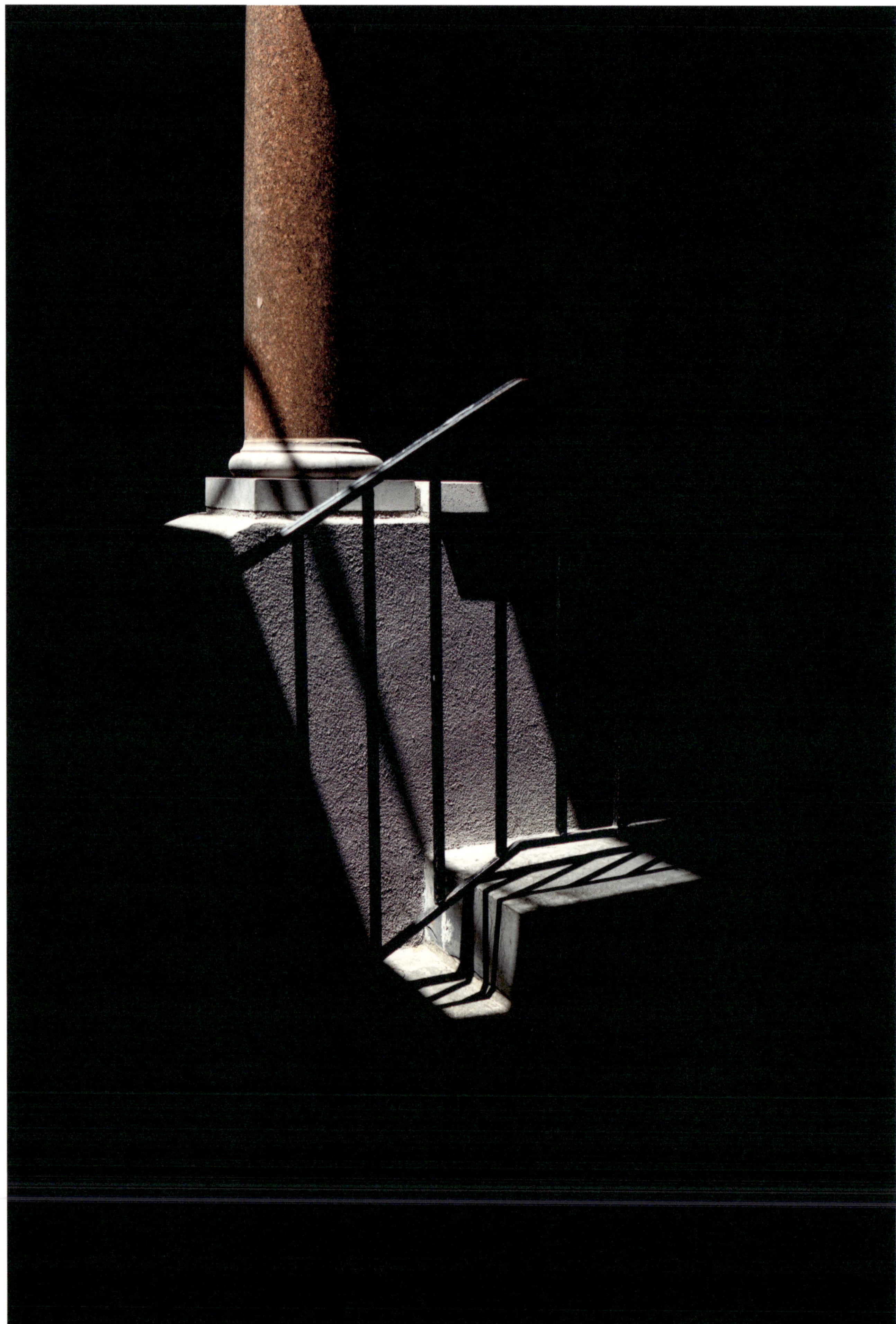

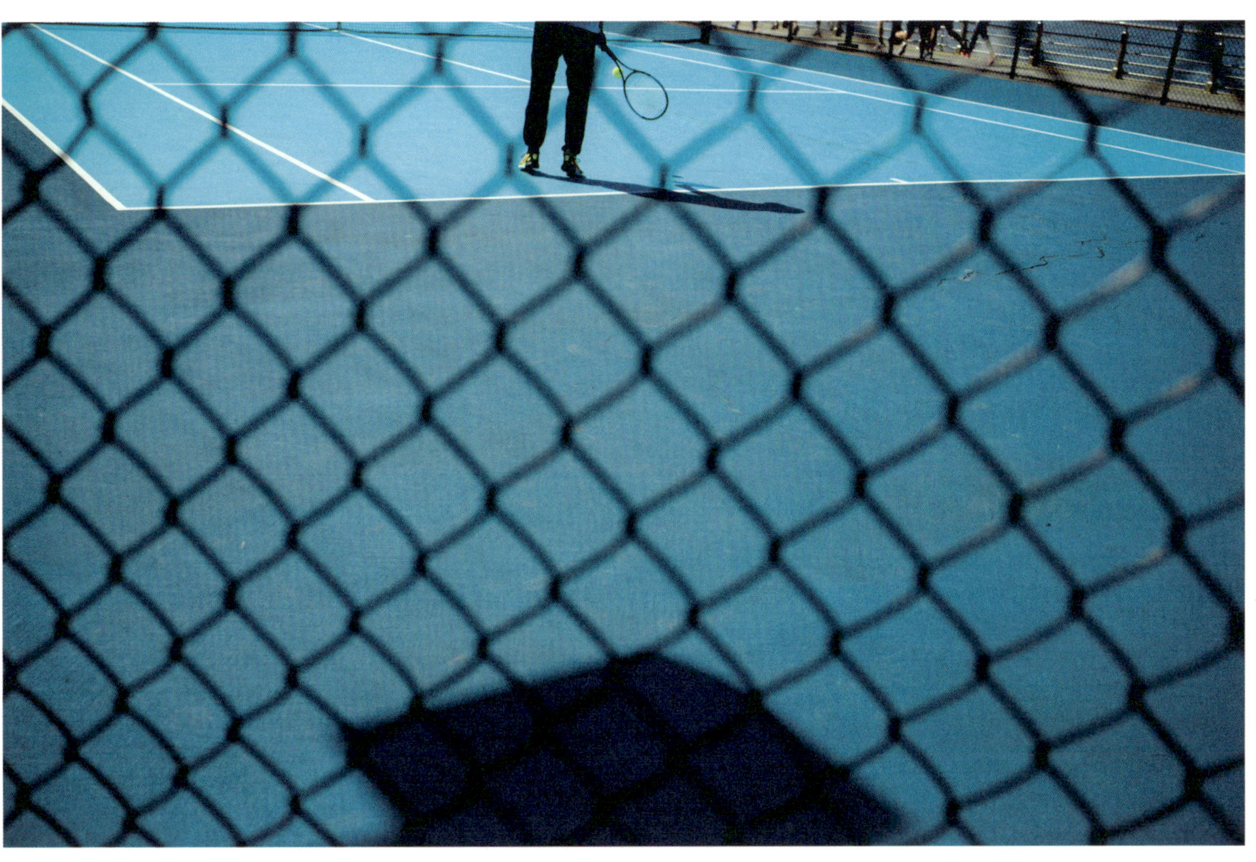

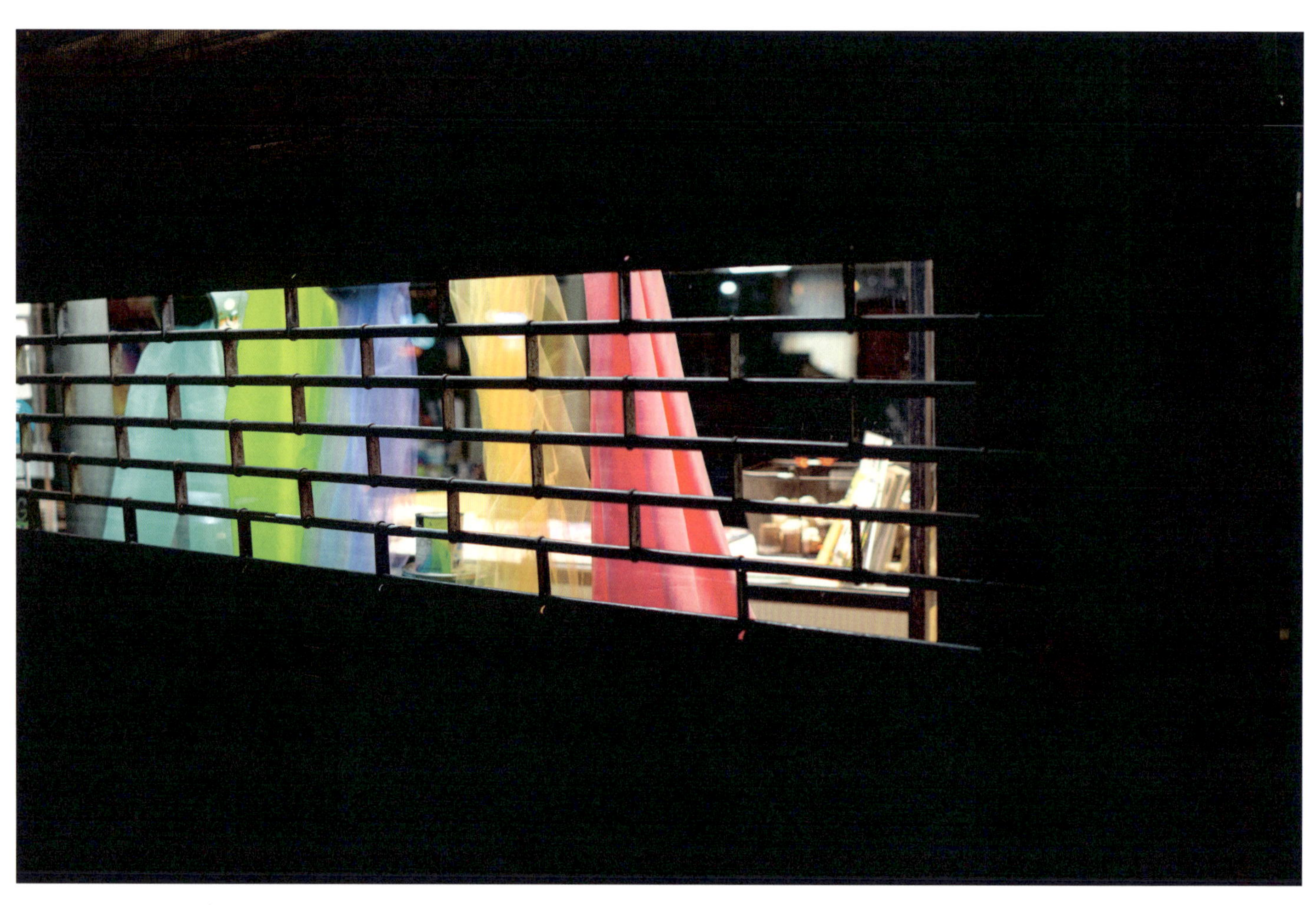

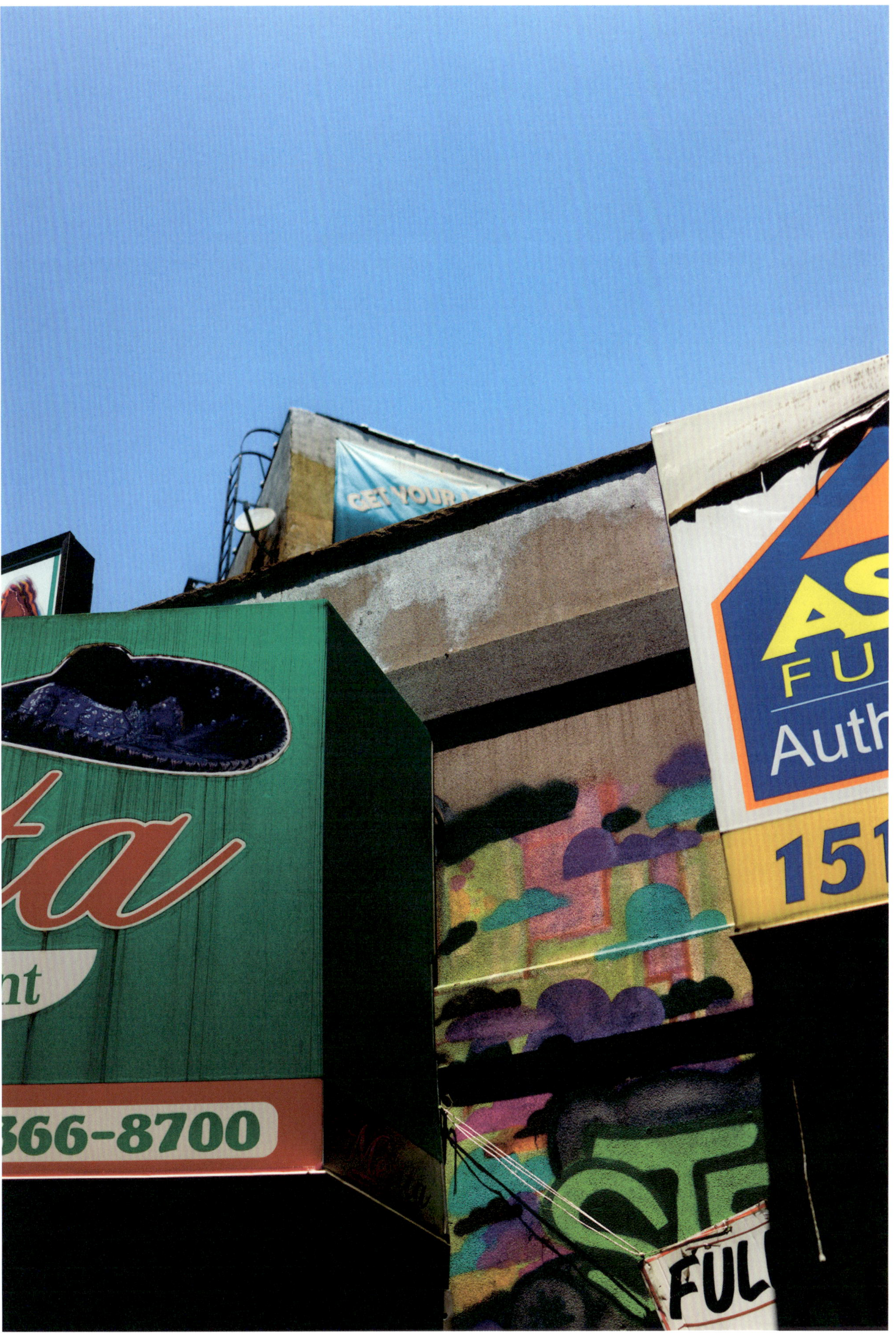
GET YOUR
ta
nt
366-8700
AS
FU
Auth
151
FUL

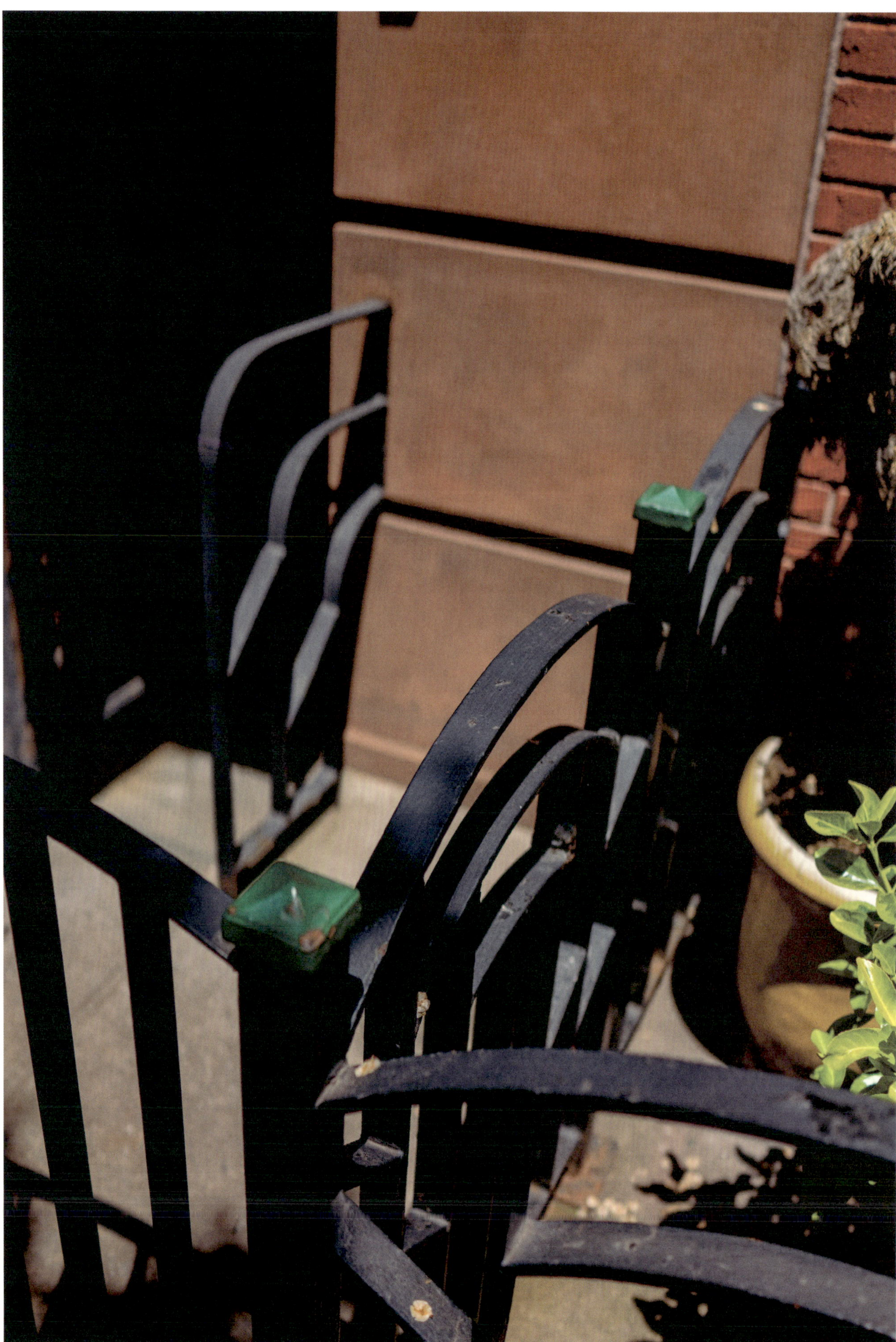

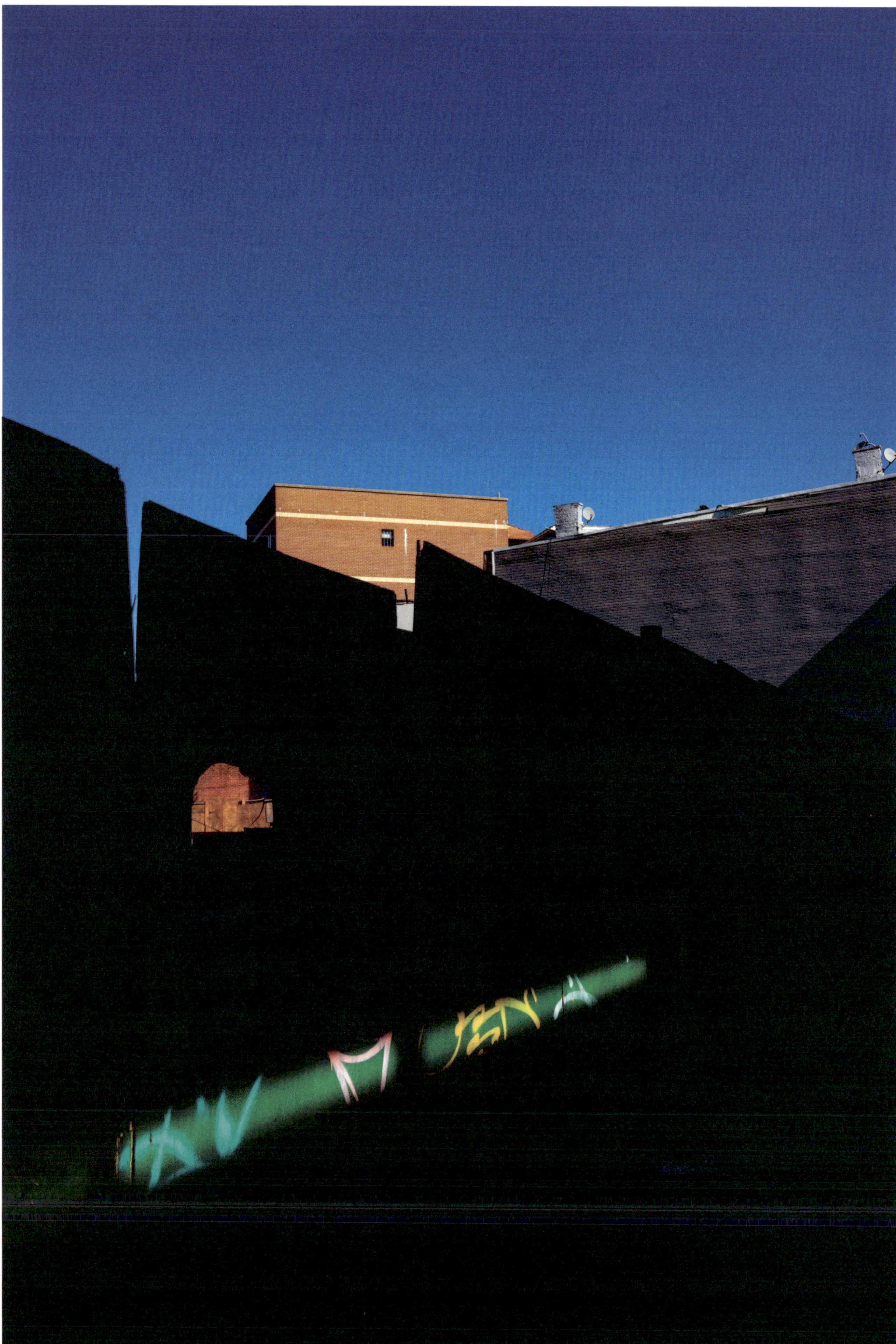

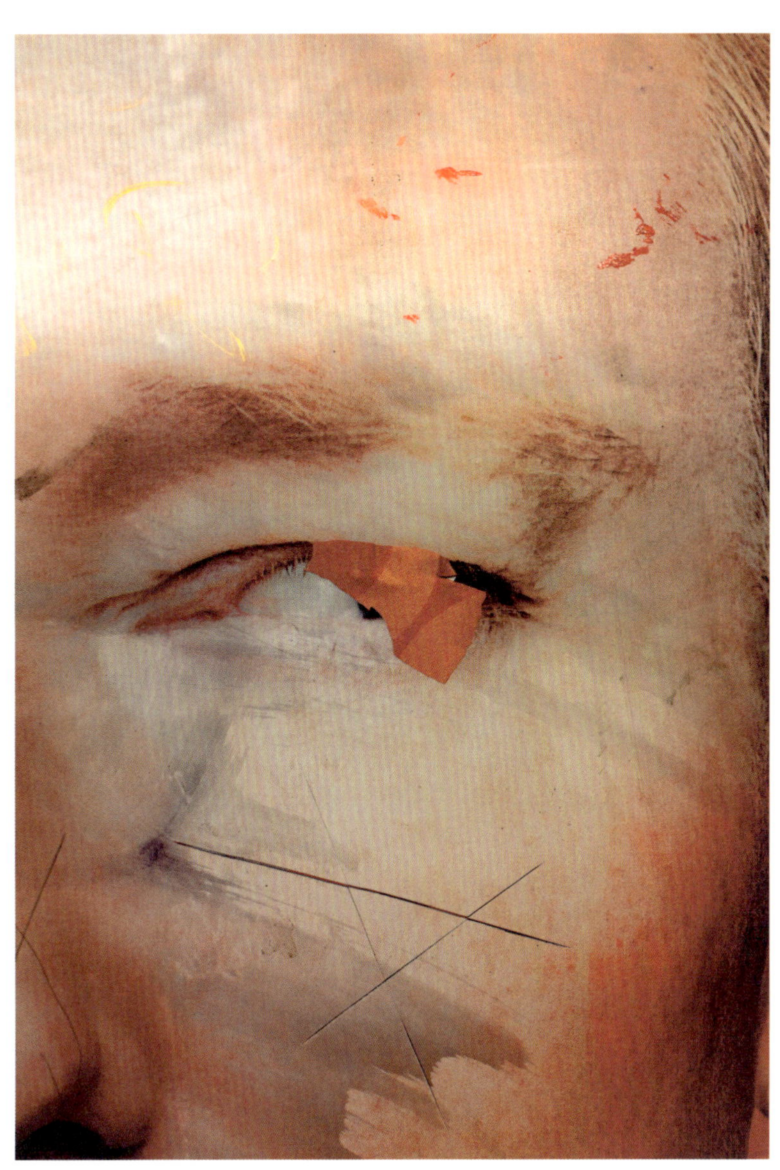

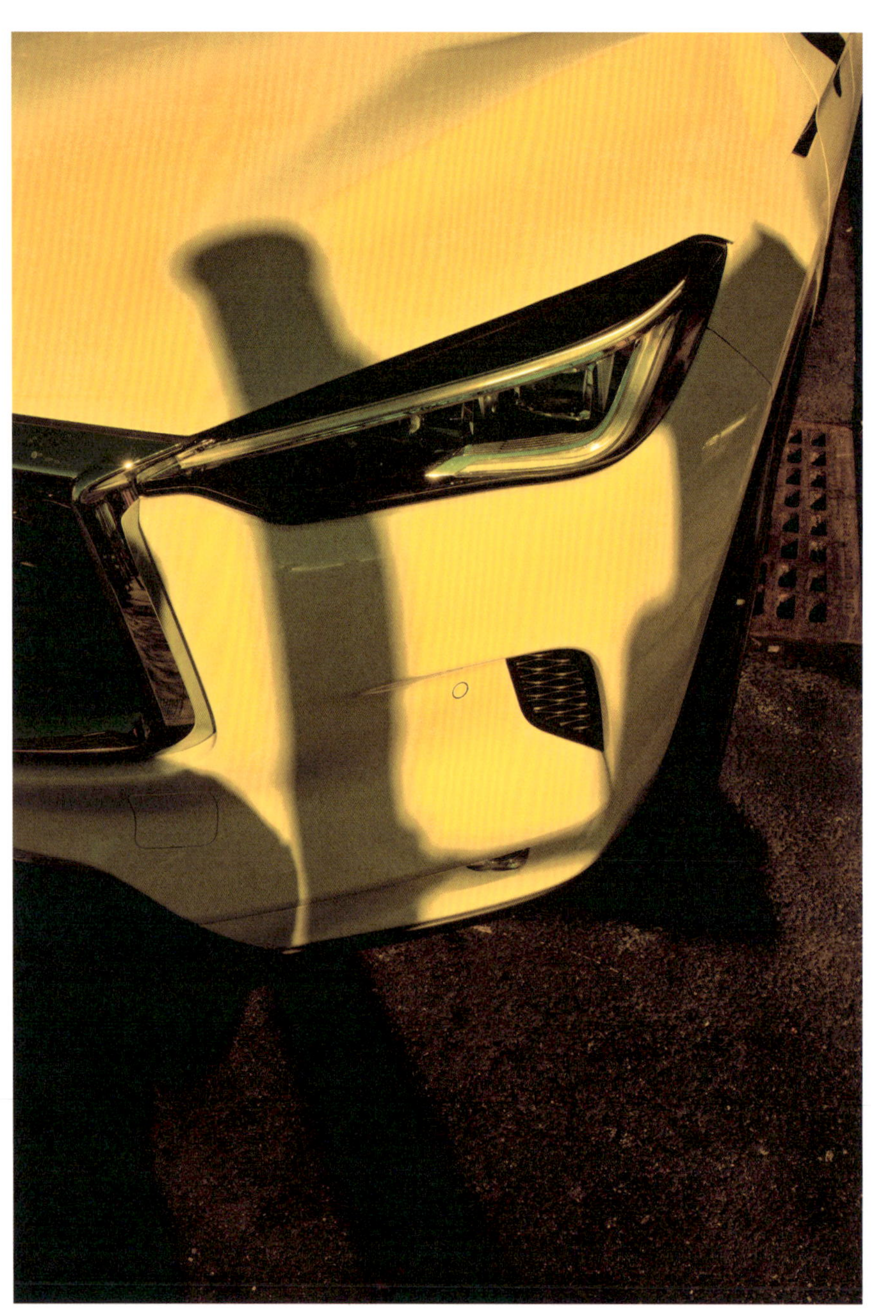

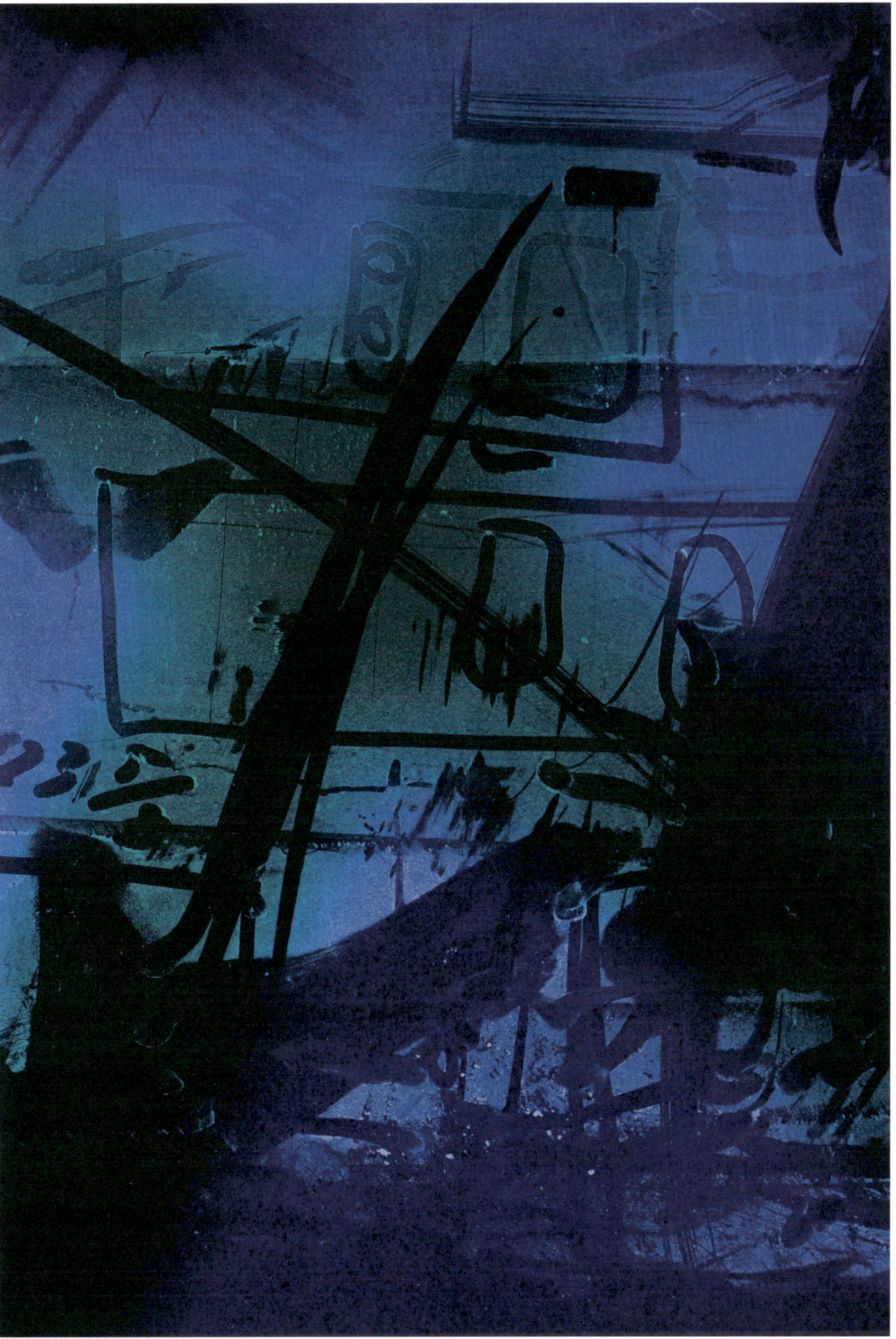

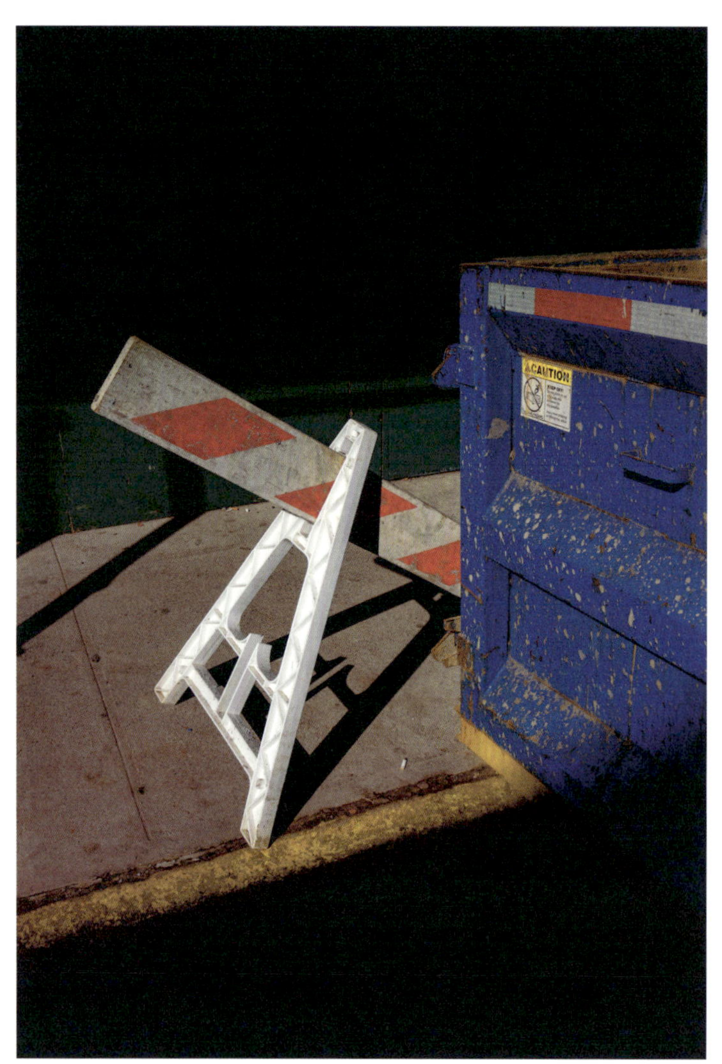
CAUTION

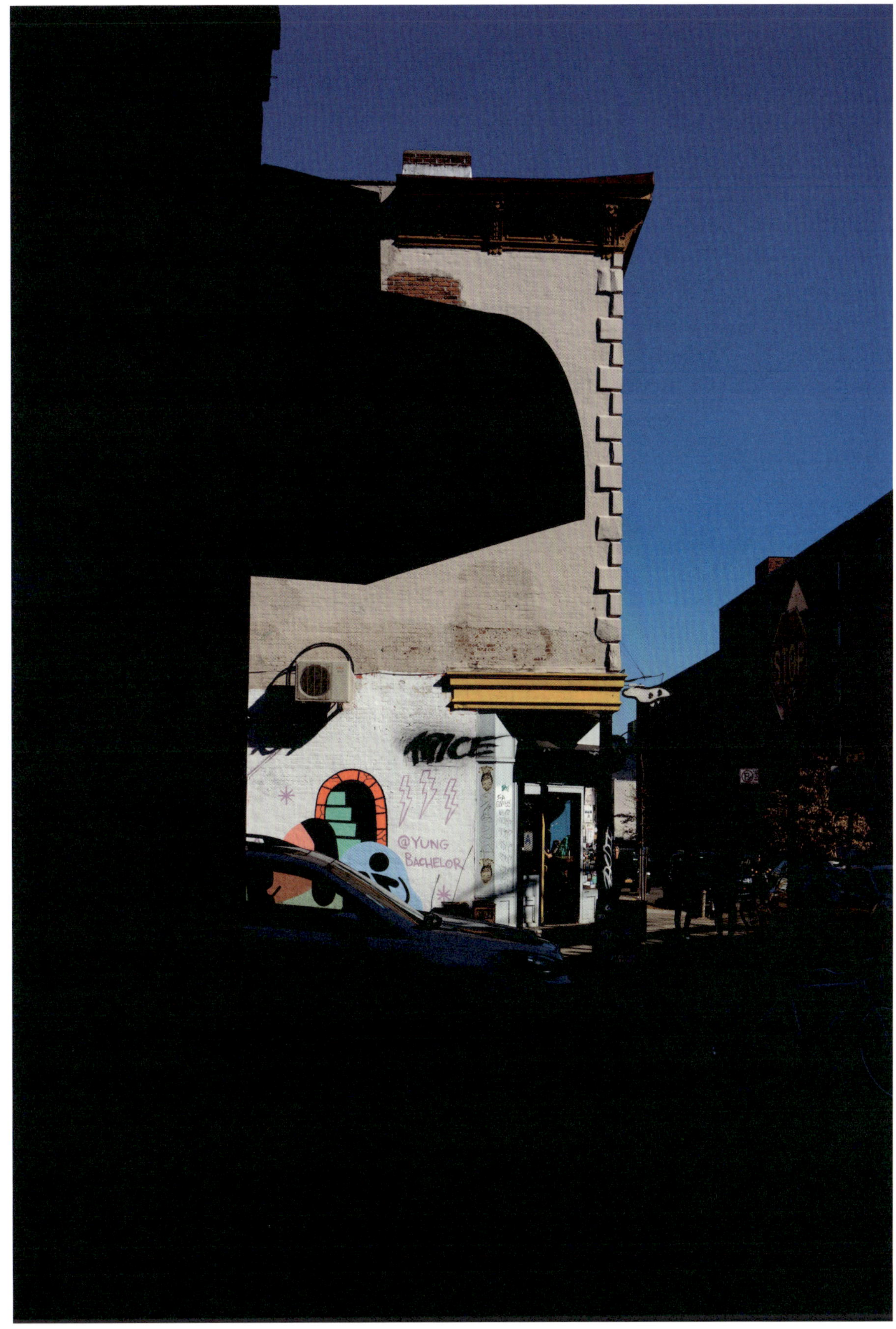
@YUNG
BACHELOR

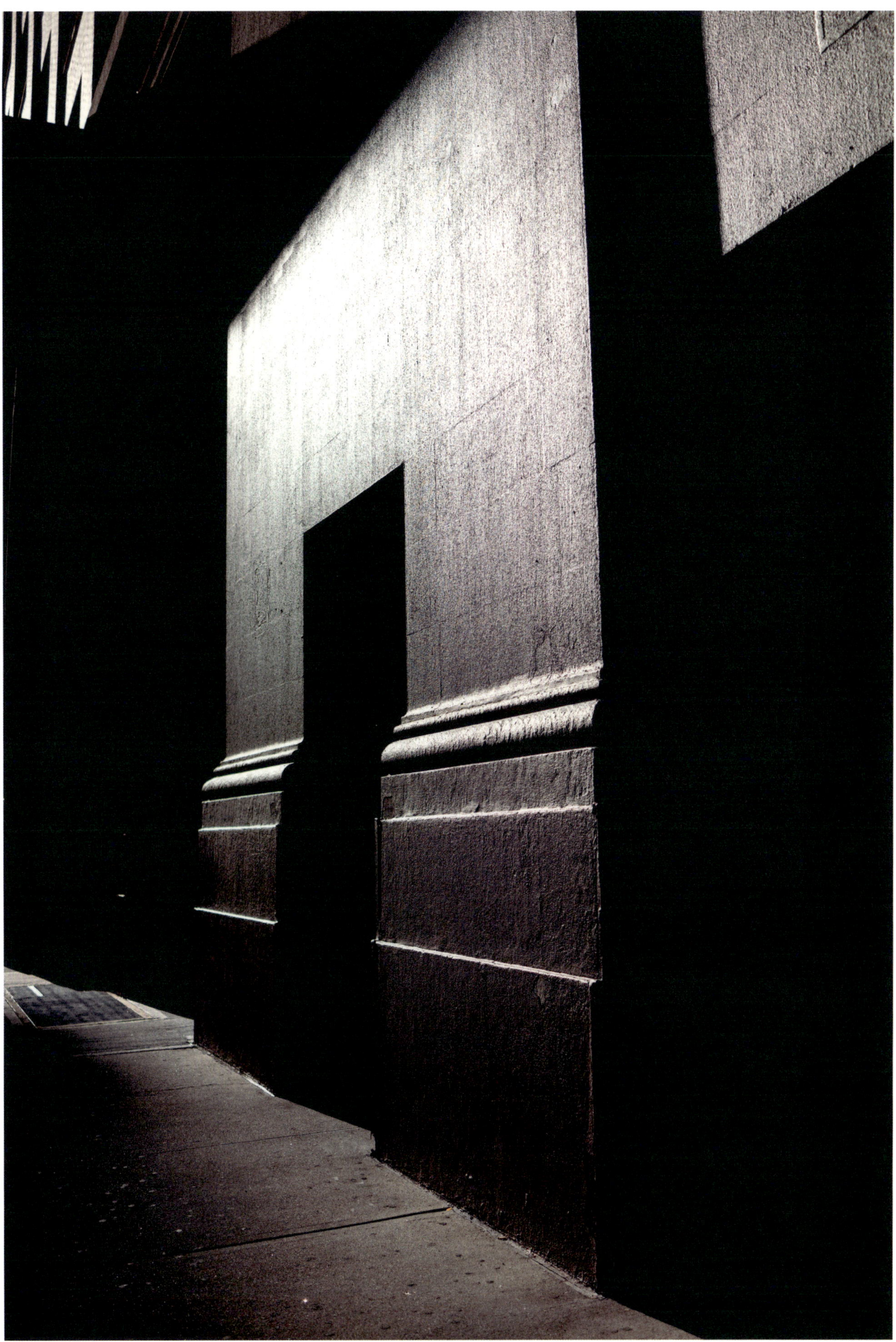

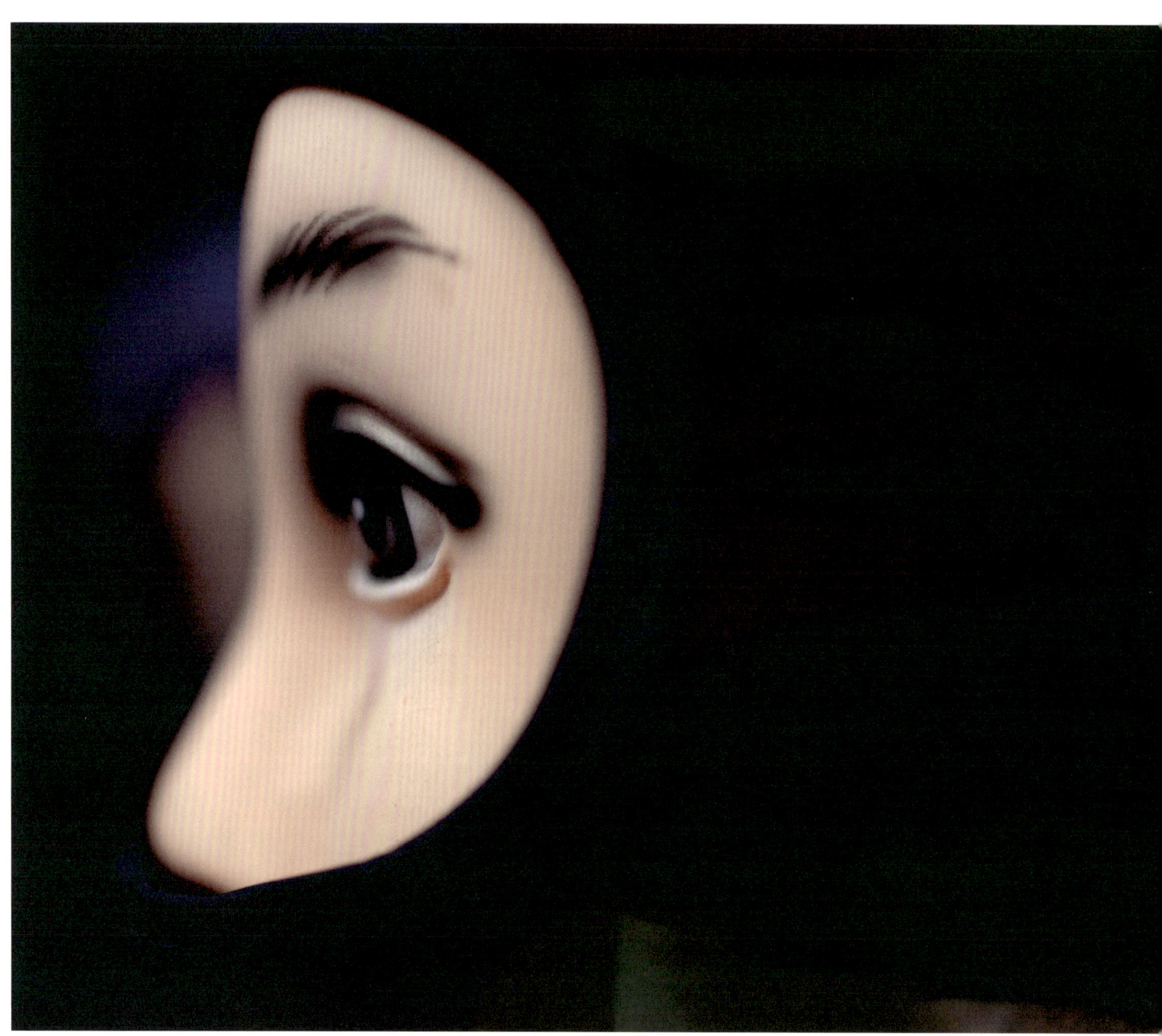

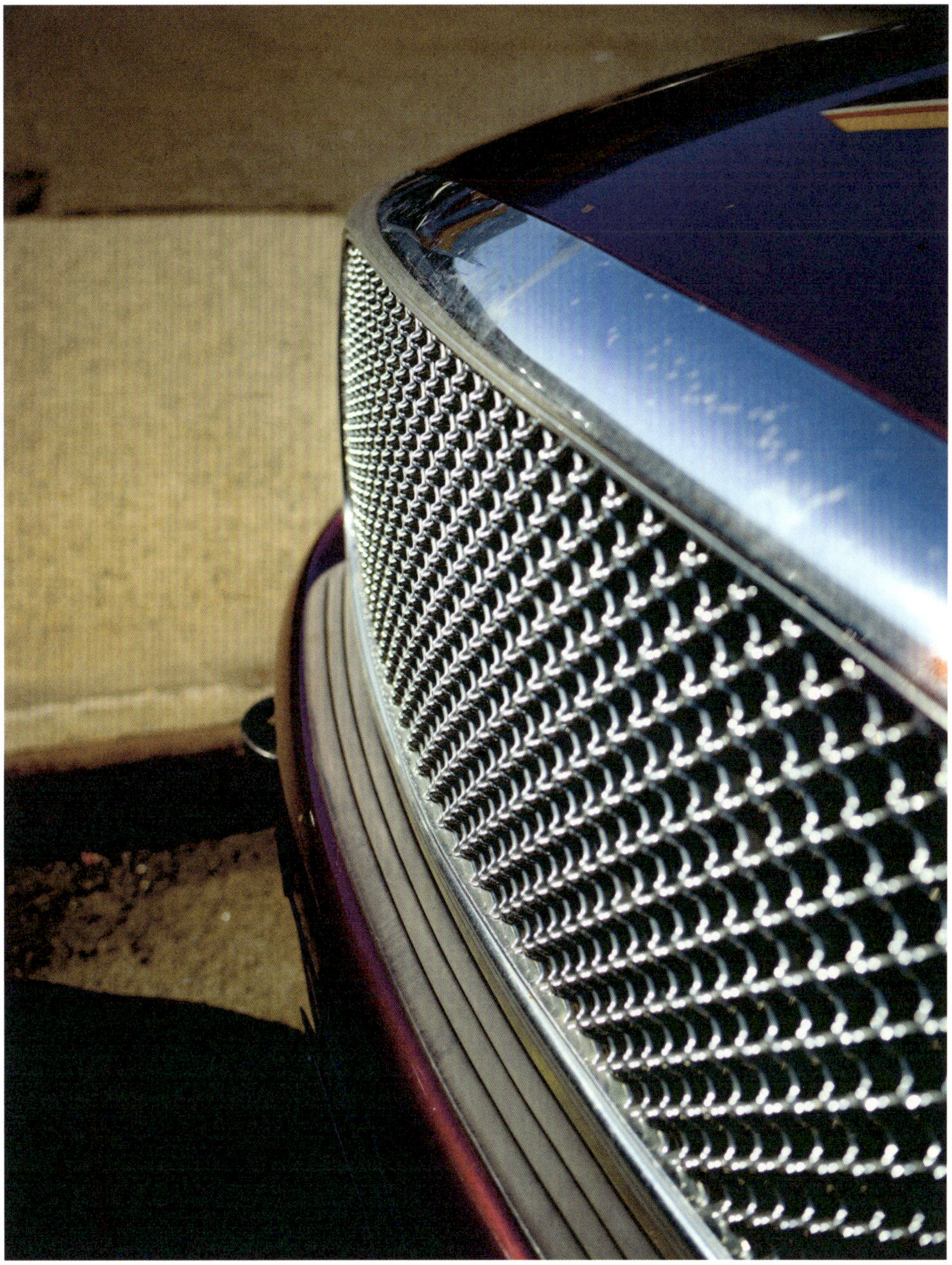

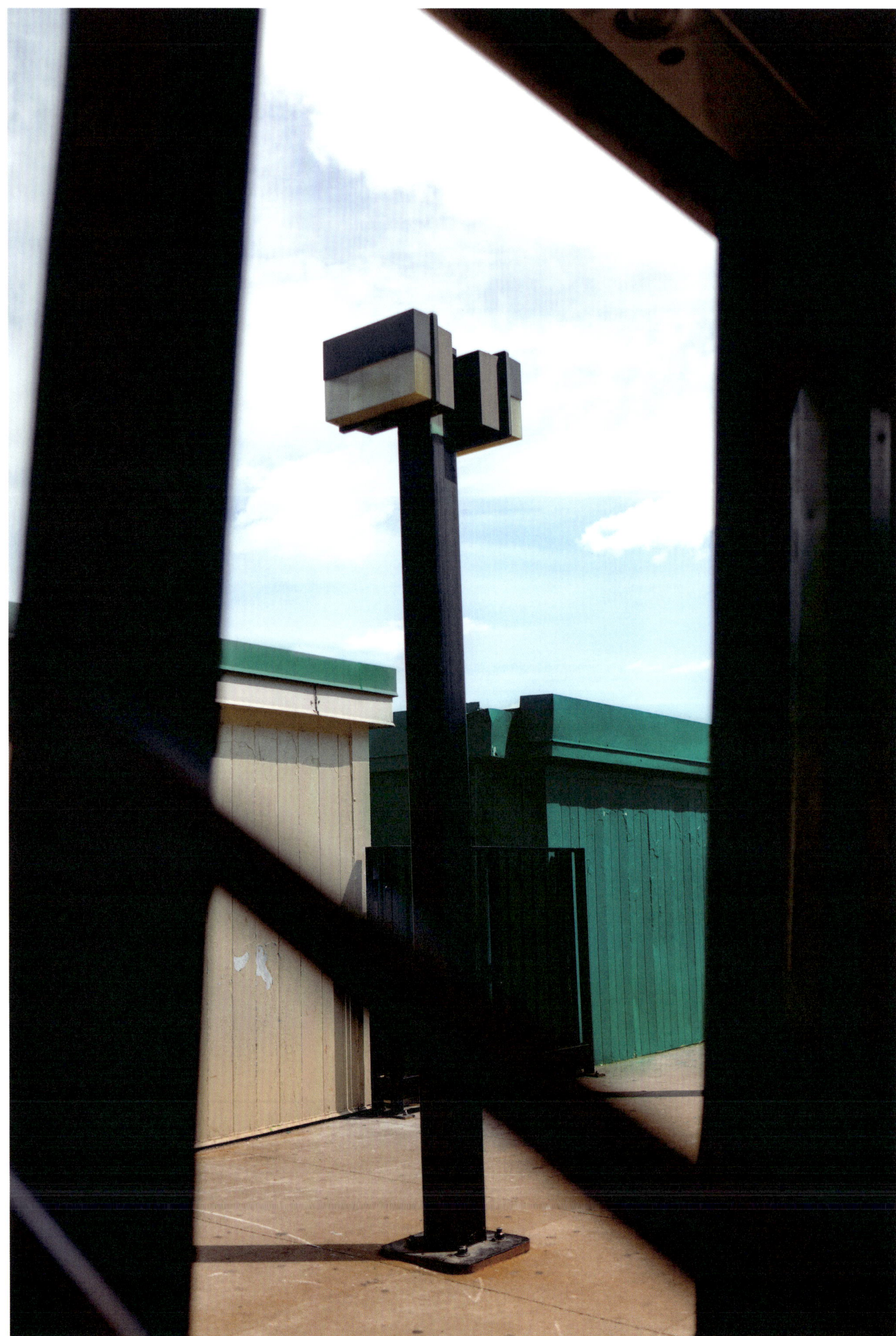

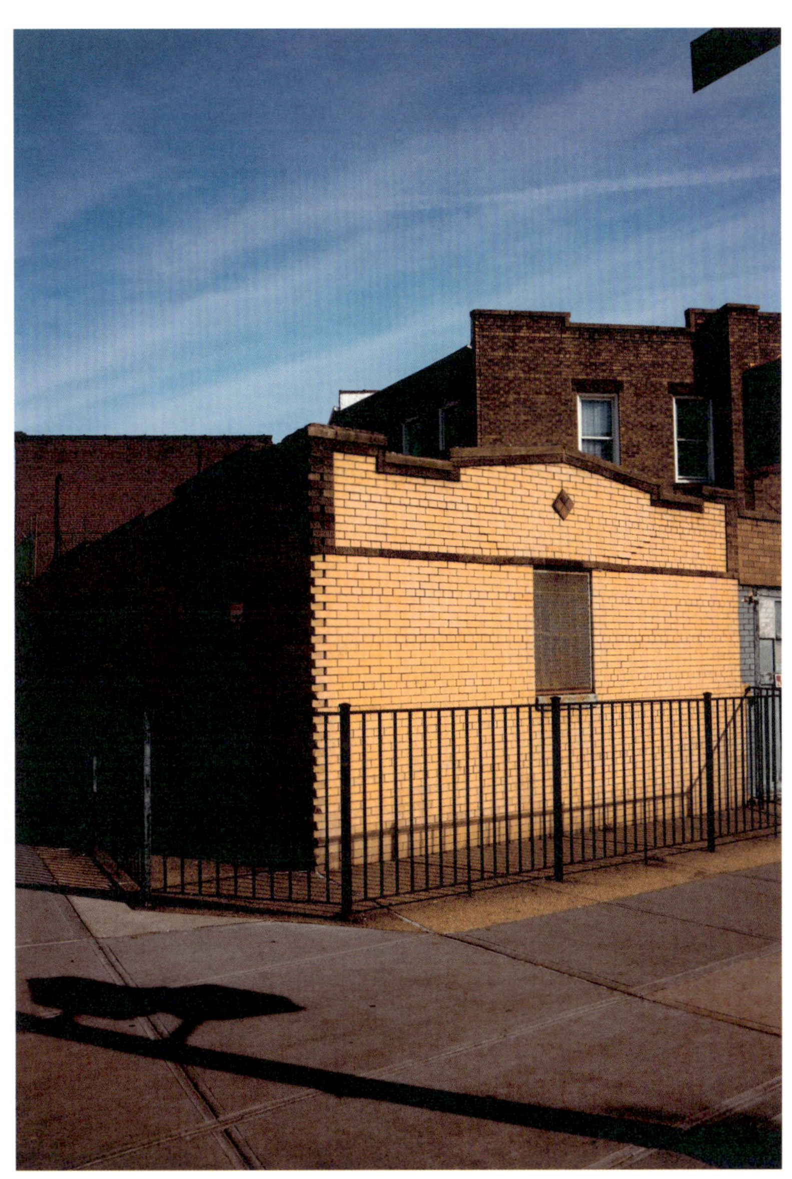

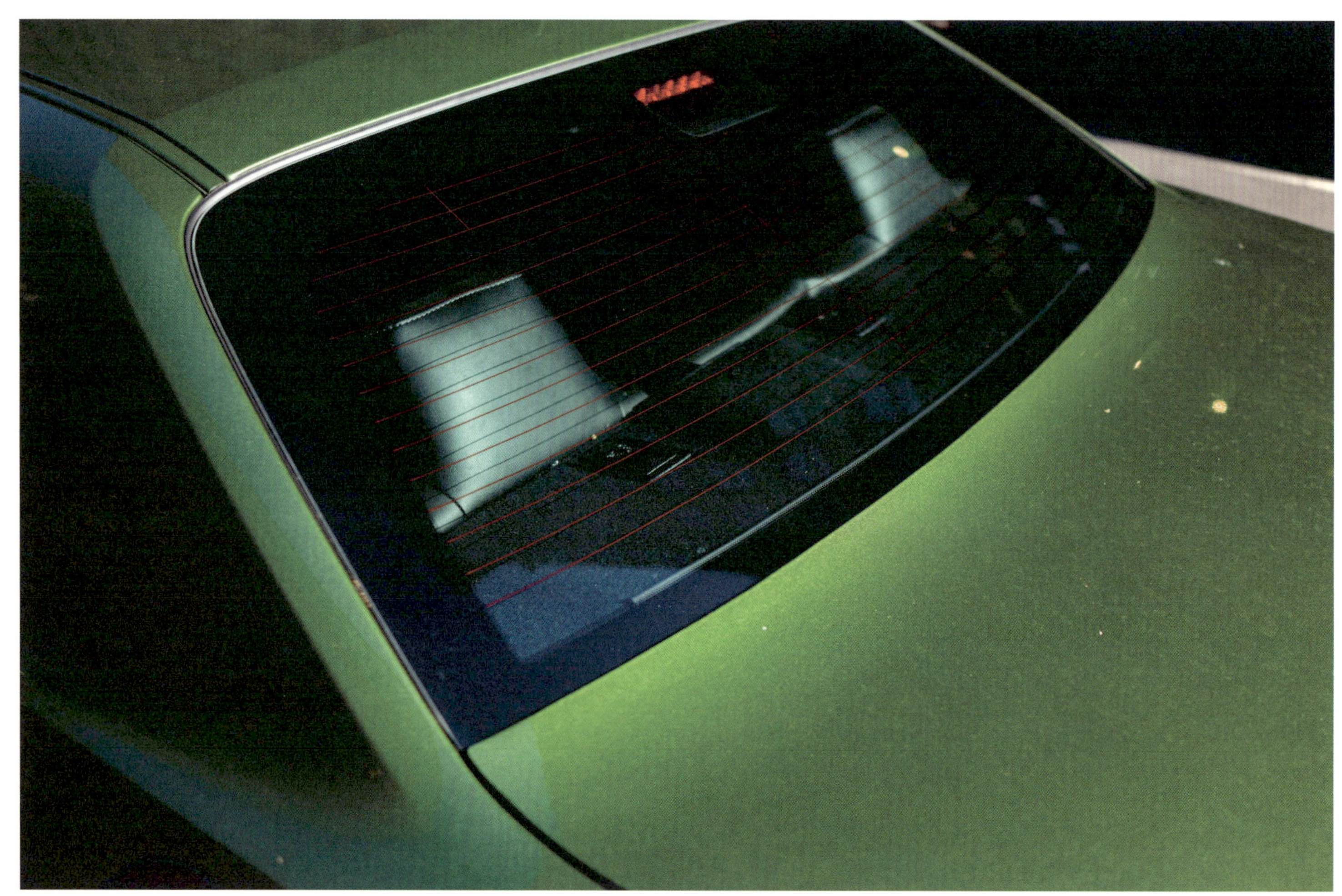

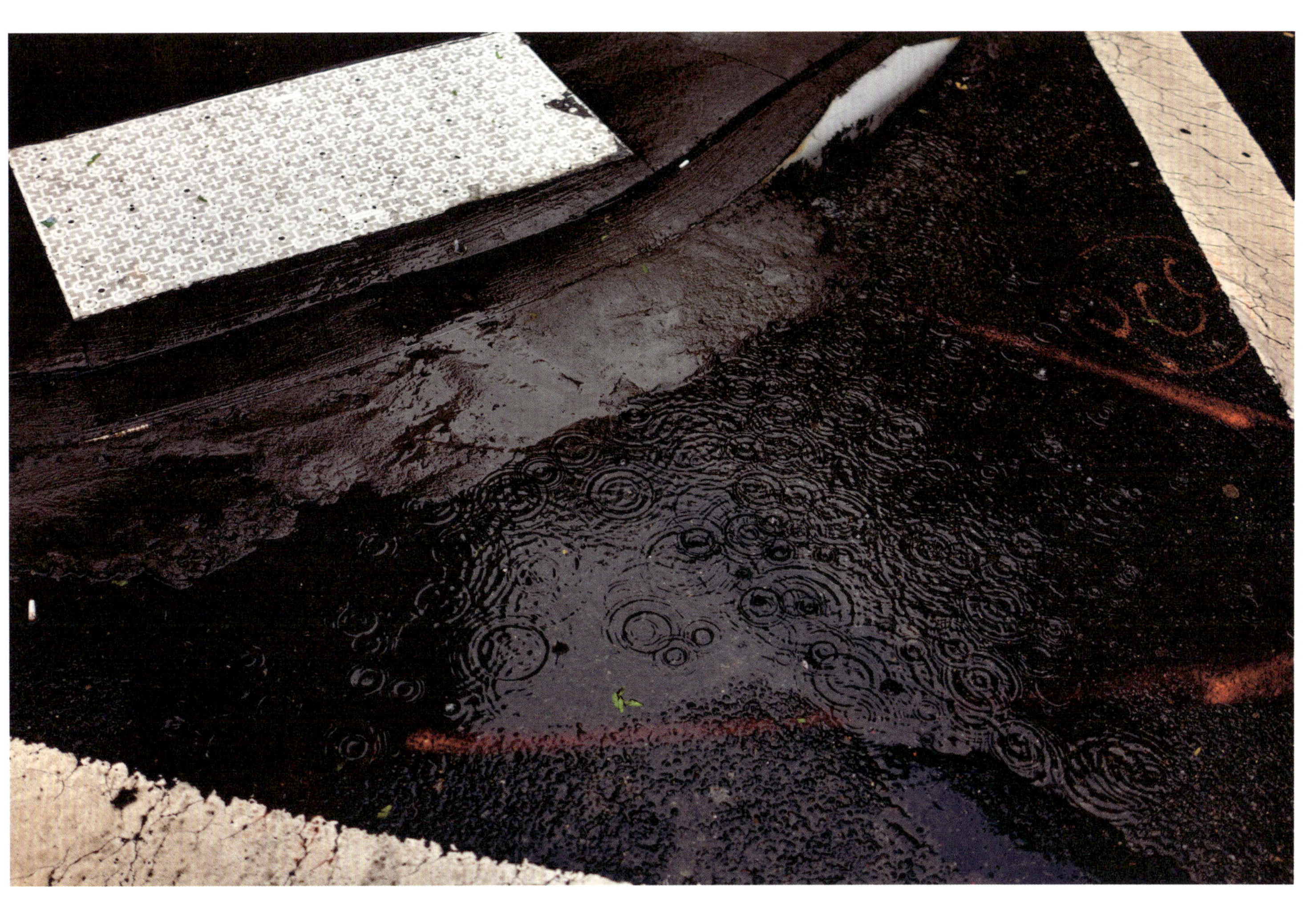

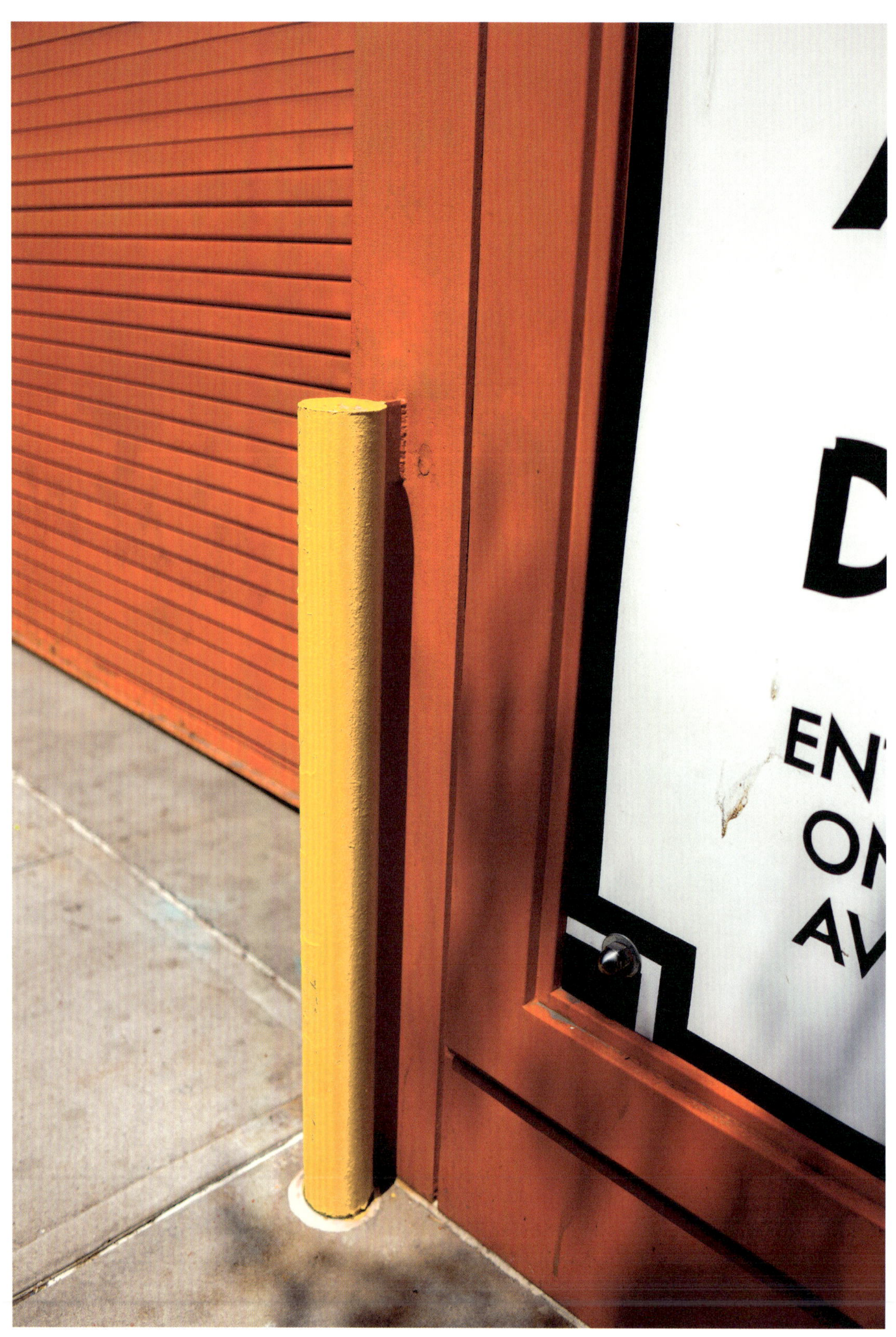

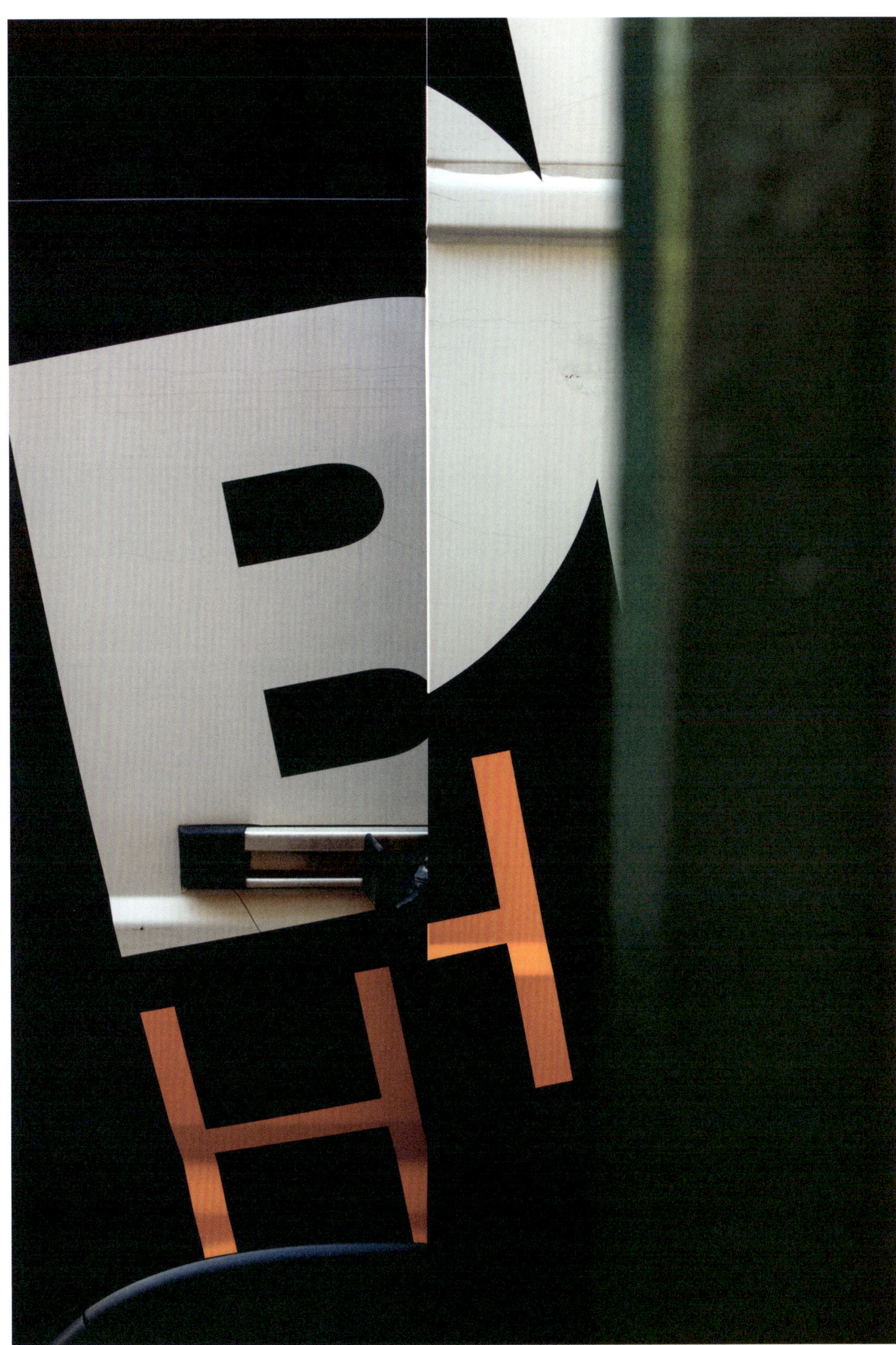

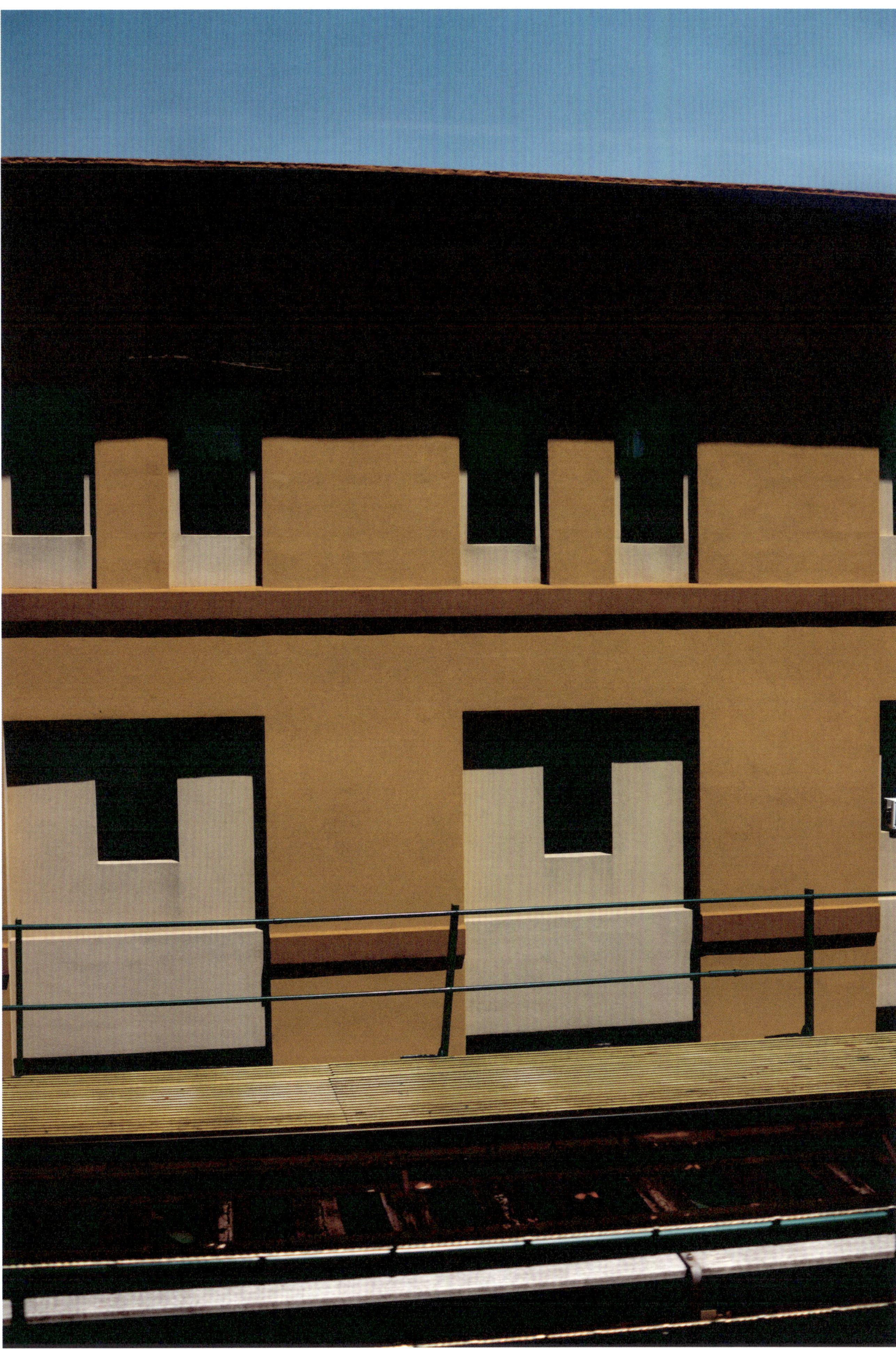

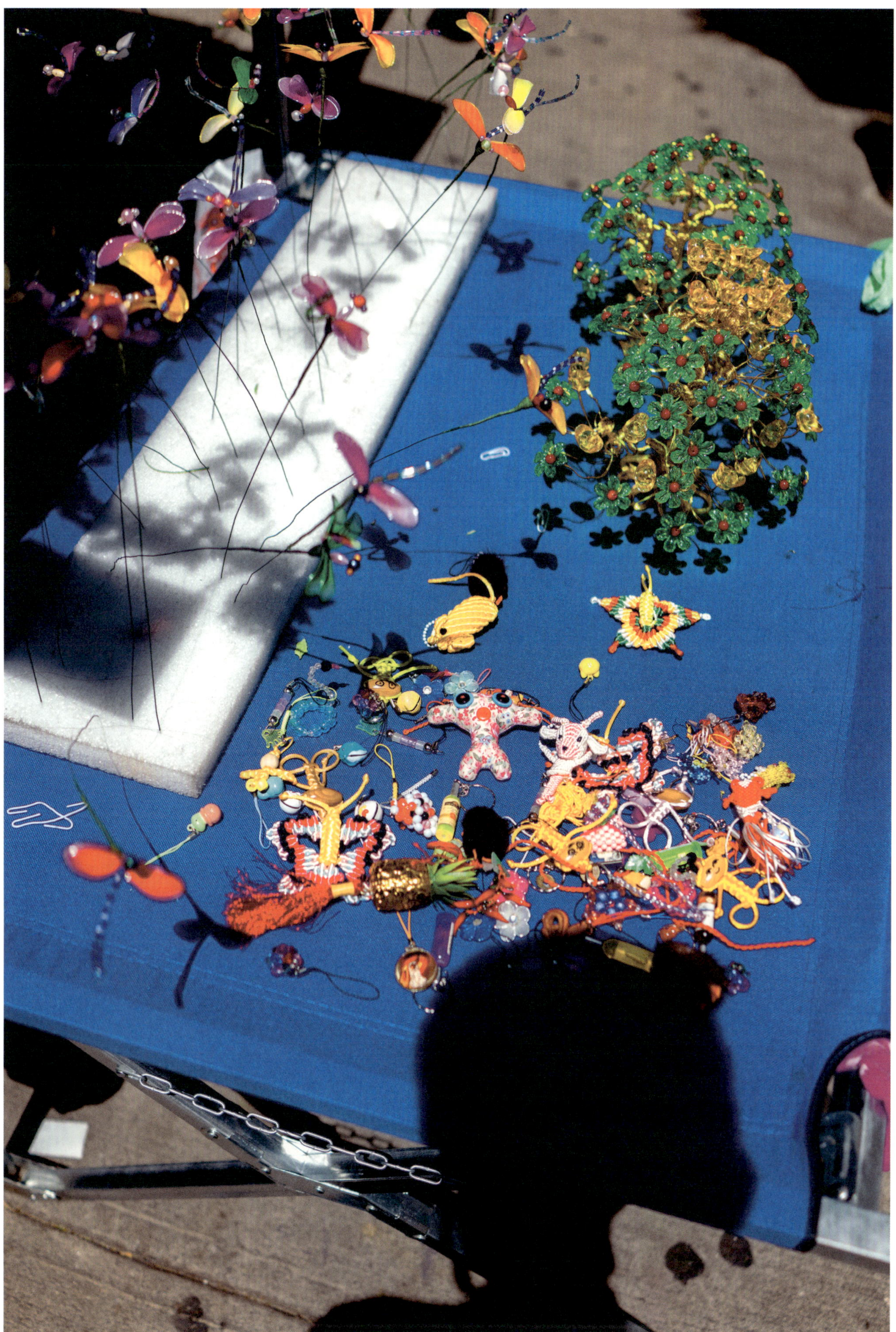

A CONVERSATION BETWEEN

TAUSIF NOOR

Let's begin by thinking about the act of looking. There is so much that can arise from a second, third, and even a fourth look. Your photography seems to pay attention to this phenomenon of looking again and looking differently at what we regard as familiar. Your new work in "Urban Spell" is full of moments that I'd call uncanny.

&

TORKIL GUDNASON

Taking the picture doesn't mean it's final. For me, it's a near-daily little exercise. I return to look at the pictures, and their meanings change during that second or third look.

My search for a new studio space, away from the one I previously had in Williamsburg, prompted "Urban Spell's" initial pictures. One day, the train didn't stop—I think it was around Jefferson Street, near Roberta's—it stopped at Halsey Street, though. I'd never been to Ridgewood before, but I came out of the stop, and I fell in love with this place. That's when I started taking the pictures; it went on for about a year and a half. Except for a handful, I took all of them in about three or four blocks of that area.

TN That element of surprise, or that spontaneity, is an important aspect of this series. It's so refreshing that even in a city like New York, such surprises still exist. The inhabitants of the city are, I think, defined at least a little by their jadedness—like "Oh, I know New York." A chance occurrence like the subway not stopping at the correct stop can lead to something incredible, and that's something I want to think about with your images. What conditions allow you as a photographer to keep that enthusiasm and energy going in your practice? How do you keep that momentum?

TG Without a doubt, the love for photography is one of the conditions, but so is curiosity. Curiosity about a new place is always stimulating. In a way, my photography is a very existential project; even though I walk down the street without walking very far, I have certainly become very conscientious of the moment and aware of movement. The rest happens instinctually. You never know whether you've had a good day or a bad day taking photographs—should you even want to make such a comparison—because it's all good in the end. Instead, you should ask yourself: how do the pictures work together, and how happy are you with them? Sometimes I'll be satisfied, and sometimes I won't be; it really is a never-ending story. I'm very blessed to be able to spend my time doing this.

TN In these photographs, and throughout your body of work, one observes a very personal relationship with the urban landscape and with architecture. I recognized some individual motifs, such as the BP gas station, which I've walked past often. But even if I hadn't recognized it, it would still be powerful because the perspective is from a very human scale. There is a one-to-one relationship between your body and what you see around yourself. The resulting image is quite inviting. No matter how far away they are, the viewer gets a sense of having been there because of the perspective and scale. This sense of proximity is, I think, very important to your work.

TG I believe that the photograph's approachable quality has to do with instinct. It's not about focusing or about anything technical. Something almost happens before that decisive moment, as Henri Cartier-Bresson called it, in that 1/60th of a second. It makes a big difference, whether it's before or after that moment, but you know when the moment is, and the photograph happens just before you know it.

TM The other aspect of that personal invitation or proximity is that your photographs seem to want to be shared. They invite another person to look at them. And because of this very personal and proximate relationship that you have with your photographs here, you're not working in a private language; instead, there is a shared language or a shared experience of the urban landscape: "I saw this, it is this way, and I want you to see it too." I wonder how you think about your audience. Do you also want to share your work with other people, show them what you've seen, or how things might be seen?

TG Absolutely. Otherwise, I'd probably feel too lonely. Everybody has a different opinion about their body of work, and everyone has personal favorites among their pictures. I don't rely on that alone because I think I just wouldn't know how to save anything. I'm too busy moving through the urban landscape—using the term "urban landscape" for the city points to how I am constantly navigating the city. You can be in nature and then go to the city fairly easily, but there is a very, very different sensibility. Deep in the urban landscape, many things are going on that rely on everyone's participation—people who have been there for a long time and those new to it. Some people love to cut across in front of the camera lens and pose, and some don't. The city has such unique energy.

TM There seem to be opportunities for things to reveal themselves or stand out to the photographer in the city. These two modes are quite apparent in this book, but what's interesting is that the things that stand out or reveal themselves might not be the most glamorous or the most iconic.

TG That's true.

TM But those things do make an impression. For instance, you have a picture of a building fragment, a stack of red bricks in front of a white wall. That's something you might walk past in New York City and think, "That's a little weird," but when you consider it for a second, it's quite striking. It's a striking contrast of colors, forms, and light and shadow. You pick up on these involuntary or unexpected relationships and juxtapositions in the city as well. You demonstrate that it's not necessarily a single thing that is striking, but a confluence of different elements that work together.

TG That's precisely the result of moving from point A to point B by walking, rather than, let's say, driving in a vehicle. You're able to see parts of the world that are not very in-your-face. I like that you used "fragments" because that's exactly what they are. These are parts that people have noticed and seen, but mostly, they are what people do not see. Hopefully, by bringing them together in this sequence, it amounts to a way of seeing differently.

TM Perhaps we could talk a little about the timeline of the production of this work. In "Urban Spell," you see snow, and you see flowers; there is an awareness of the passage of time because the environment is also changing. The city is a very dynamic space not only because you're thinking of all these different fragments working together, but because these elements are also changing. How long have you worked on this series, and what have you seen in terms of transformation and change?

TG I've worked on this series for about a year or two. Some days are more productive than others, but I work on a near-daily basis. I print the images as small work prints, about 8 × 10 inch. I spread them out on a table, and sometimes there's absolutely no doubt that one image suits another. But having that luxury of time to live with them and return to them is instrumental in our day and age, in which everything occurs not only on a small monitor, everything is also very rushed. I enjoy the luxury of laying them out in a large space, but also of having the time to think.

TM The practice of going back to think about and rethink your images allows for connections you might not have made initially to emerge, just from the relationships between one photograph, or a set of photographs, to another. Things don't have to happen in the same way, chronologically or even spatially. It seems this project has allowed you to think about your relationship with the city and about how the city's different elements have a relationship with one another, which is fantastic.

TG It's not a linear way of thinking at all. You can come in with the best intentions and be as professional—a word that I don't like to use—as you want, but in my experience, there's more to it than that. It's a process, and all of a sudden, something can come in, like the new kid on the block, and you might have to start all over again, or you might have to kill your darlings.

TM You have gained quite a bit of experience working in photography over the years, and you've worked in a range of styles. I want to ask what advice you would give to someone starting as a photographer, but perhaps differently: what is the advice you've received that has helped you during all this time? Which things have stood the test of time, even as the field and your interests were changing?

TG It would be to follow your heart because the rest will follow—and to realize and recognize your love, above all. Of course, we all have dreams that need to find a place in our lives, but there's always something that comes before everything else. In my case, I love photography. But photography by itself is not enough. I think creating the curiosity and proximity—the space, the time, the relationships—all point to a need in yourself and are present in certain inspirational moments. Those moments can be in a book, in the theater, meeting people; they can be like the conversation we're having right now. Returning to the urban environment of New York: it is full of this kind of inspiration, both good and bad. I wouldn't say to people who are starting that it is glamorous, but it's important to identify the urge you have and learn how to work with that.

TM Purpose and intention, as you allude to, are important, but as you've also said, it's equally important to be open, and I think the urban environment helps us achieve that. It can force us to open ourselves up to chance and spontaneity, as we discussed previously, but it's also important to think about our influences. There are a very long tradition and history of street photography. Some urban photographers have taken iconic images of New York and generally of urban environments, such as Lee Friedlander. Are there any precedents or influences that are particularly important to you?

TG Yes. I've met Lee Friedlander personally, and he's extraordinary and a big inspiration. I look at many photographers' work; their work and influence remains with me because I'm interested in their styles. I saw a book the other day by Henri Cartier-Bresson with pictures he took in China in 1949. He spent a couple of years there on two occasions. His work is extraordinary and embraces so much of this sense of openness and spontaneity that we're discussing. His photos are mostly of people, and they exemplify the tradition of street photojournalism. I was always interested in still lifes, in painting but also by people like Irving Penn. My interest in architecture couples with these interests, and I'm lucky to have an eye for that. But we're all different, so, walking down the same street, we might capture something completely different. I'm glad you recognized my interest in architecture. These pictures are from Ridgewood; we're not talking about Brasilia, where you're served modernist architecture on a silver platter. But for me, this is almost better because the people are extraordinary. I love them. They're unpretentious and going about their lives, but you can connect with everyone. I know my entire street already, which is fantastic because, as you said, New Yorkers have a reputation for being jaded or unfriendly. I'm so happy to find this inspiration in Ridgewood, rather than Williamsburg, and continue with that. I actually created a little book called "Ridgewood" with no text, just fragments; it has many pictures on each page that were laid out very freely. That was maybe the groundwork for this series, or at least the hors d'oeuvres to this dish.

TN It just goes to show that looking back at your own work can allow your practice to take new directions. The series also shows that there isn't necessarily a formula, which is quite a liberating perspective on photography. All of the things that come together—subject, composition, lighting, color— sometimes come together by chance.

TG It often is by chance. When we think about the switch to digital photography and tools like the iPhone, these developments have a lot to do with this chance, whether we like it or not. Because of these developments, there has been an enormous output—we are getting used to seeing and expecting to see a lot of pictures.

TN On that technical note, how do you approach your photography now—are you taking pictures with your camera and your phone simultaneously? How do you negotiate these different kinds of technology?

TG I had my moment with the iPhone, but it's just not technically as great as a camera. When the iPhones first came out, they were more geared for video and depth of field, so in a way, they were predictable. I like cameras that can do 4 × 5 or 8 × 10 inch images, which have been around since the beginning of photography, more or less. And iPhones are convenient and easy to use, but for the past five or six years, at least, I've carried a camera with me all the time. It's become almost second nature.

TN That's quite interesting too, because while the iPhone is a kind of camera that you might always have with you, carrying a digital or analog camera all the time also trains you in the way of looking, even with all the experience you've had. It's an apparatus that trains you to look, as much as it captures images.

TG And that's where the iPhone comes in, but I'm beyond that now. The camera hanging around my neck is my new iPhone.

TN Learning how to look at and read images is one of the most important skills, if not the most important skill for a critic, and that means looking closely and carefully. There's a nice relationship between looking, taking images, and editing. As you said earlier, the process of editing is also the process of drawing connections, looking for similarities, differences, and productive frictions, all of which are important in the photographer's practice and contribute to the viewer's experience. In the "Urban Spell" series, there are images with different sizes, different formats and layouts, different amounts of white space. It's quite exciting to see that in a book because there are some unexpected combinations.

TG That's what you've been seeing in photobooks for the past four or five years, and there's been an explosion of photobooks. There are events, such as the Printed Matter Art Book Fair at MoMA PS1, which have grown so much in popularity. About ten years ago, there were only a few art book sellers, Printed Matter was one of them. Now there's an enormous interest in this alternative way of seeing and interest in printed material as opposed to digital monitors. This is the way we stake our claims, our way of communicating, even though it's not mainstream, and it's not very commercial. Some of these books are even only made as an edition of a few hundred.

TN I think art books help people see differently, giving them the license or confidence to say that their landscapes, the things they see in their neighborhoods, matter. And it doesn't have to be just in New York City—all these different landscapes, like William Eggleston's photos of the South, or wherever actually, can be viewed in interesting and unique ways, and captured in exciting formats. That's why I love the title "Urban Spell." It conveys the idea that magic is possible in one's surroundings, that it exists everywhere. Your pictures were shot in New York, but that magic doesn't have to be in New York.

TG I think it is happening in many places, not just in one place or in one way. Magic is occurring because people are moving around more and recognizing all the great cities. The urban environment is a product of humanity. It's always interesting, and it's ever-changing, often so quickly and in so many different ways. It's a negotiation between the different roles and responsibilities that we all have in this environment. In the end, if you can help people and share what you create, that's the ultimate goal. Artists are needed to keep this magic going. I would go so far as to say that they are responsible for keeping it going.

Tausif Noor is a critic, curator, and graduate student working in the fields of modern and contemporary global art. His writing can be found in Artforum, frieze, ArtAsiaPacific, BOMB, and various other magazines, as well as in artist catalogues for Alex Da Corte (KARMA, 2019) and the India Habitat Centre in New Delhi. He has previously worked at the Imperial War Museum in London, the Whitney Museum, and the Institute of Contemporary Art at the University of Pennsylvania.

Thank you to Matthias Kliefoth, Christian Boros, Tausif Noor, and Madeleine Thomas.
A special thank you to my family.

Concept, Photography, Design
Torkil Gudnason
torkilgudnasonstudio.com

Graphic Design
Manuel Tayarani, DISTANZ Verlag

Text
Tausif Noor

Copy Editing
Katerine Niedinger

Production Management
DISTANZ Verlag

Printing and Binding
optimal media GmbH, Roebel/Mueritz

Distribution
Edel Germany GmbH
www.edel.com
international-books@edel.com

ISBN 978-3-95476-356-6
Printed in Germany

Published by
DISTANZ Verlag
www.distanz.de